READER'S DIGEST

EARTH'S RICHES

URANIUM IN CANADA

Small amounts of uranium are found throughout the Earth's crust and mantle, but in certain places the movement of hot fluids has transported and concentrated rich deposits of its ore. The Athabasca Basin in northern Saskatchewan has large deposits of high-grade uranium ore beneath an area of 100 000 km². They mostly lie within 600 m of the surface and so are easy to reach. The basin's two active mines, at McClean Lake and McArthur River, account for around a third of the world's total production of mined uranium. The McArthur River mine has large reserves of particularly high-grade ore with a concentration of 20 per cent of the metal within the ore. Uranium's main use is to fuel nuclear power stations.

URANIUM

Canada

North America

USA

COAL

Continental Crust

COAL

BLACK THUNDER IN WYOMING

Clouds of coal dust explode skywards during blasting at the world's largest open-cast coal mine – the Black Thunder in Wyoming, USA. Plants that lived and died in swampy deltas millions of years ago laid down the Earth's coal riches. Layers of their remains were buried and compacted, eventually turning into coal. The Black Thunder seam is part of the Wyodak seam beneath huge tracts of Wyoming, Montana and Dakota. Since 1977, it has yielded nearly 1000 million tonnes of coal.

HARVESTING SUN IN CALIFORNIA

The world's largest solar power facility is Kramer Junction in the Mojave Desert. An array of parabolic troughs covering 400 hectares concentrates the Sun's energy to generate enough electricity to supply about 150 000 homes. Although solar energy can be tapped anywhere, places with a lot of sunshine hours are obviously the best choice. In recent years, small-scale installations, such as solar panels on roofs to heat water, have been joined by large-scale solar plants. Globally, there are now more than 2 million m² of parabolic trough collectors.

WER

SOUTH AFRICAN GOLD

More than half of all the gold ever mined is from the Witwatersrand Basin near Johannesburg. The Witwatersrand 'reef' is a seam of rock about 11 km thick and covering an area 270 km by 100 km, where gold washed out of ancient mountains settled among river gravels, shale and sandstone sediments. The seam dips sharply and extraction, which began in 1886, has always relied on deep-shaft mines. As more gold is extracted, the mines go deeper – some are 4 km deep.

A PANORAMA OF RICHES

Earth's riches are to be found all over the globe, but certain places – some of them highlighted here – are especially well endowed. From the deserts of Arabia, sitting on vast oil wealth, to the frozen tundra of Siberia with the largest onshore gas field, they include some of the most inhospitable regions on the planet. Some of these concentrations are the result of tectonic activity within the Earth's crust, such as the fabled silver mines of Mexico; others, such as the ruby-rich gravels of Myanmar (Burma), are the result of combinations of factors, including the weathering of rock and the flow of rivers. Wherever they are, the ingenuity of mankind has sought them out and found ways of extracting them.

SOLAR POWER

Gulf of California

SILVER

Mexico

Gulf of Mexico

Mesozoic Sedimentary Rock

Tertiary Sedimentary Rock

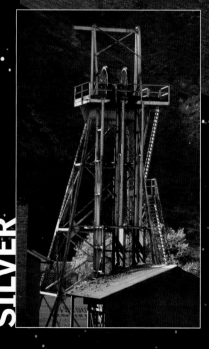

MEXICO'S SILVER Mexico has long been the leader in silver production, with a series of high-grade deposits along its 800 km *faja de plata* ('silver belt') in the Sierra Madre mountains of Chihuaha province. This is part of a larger geological formation that includes the Andes and other high-grade silver deposits as far south as Peru and Bolivia. Silver and other ores – notably copper – formed here as a result of tectonic activity around the Pacific 'Ring of Fire'.

SOLAR PO

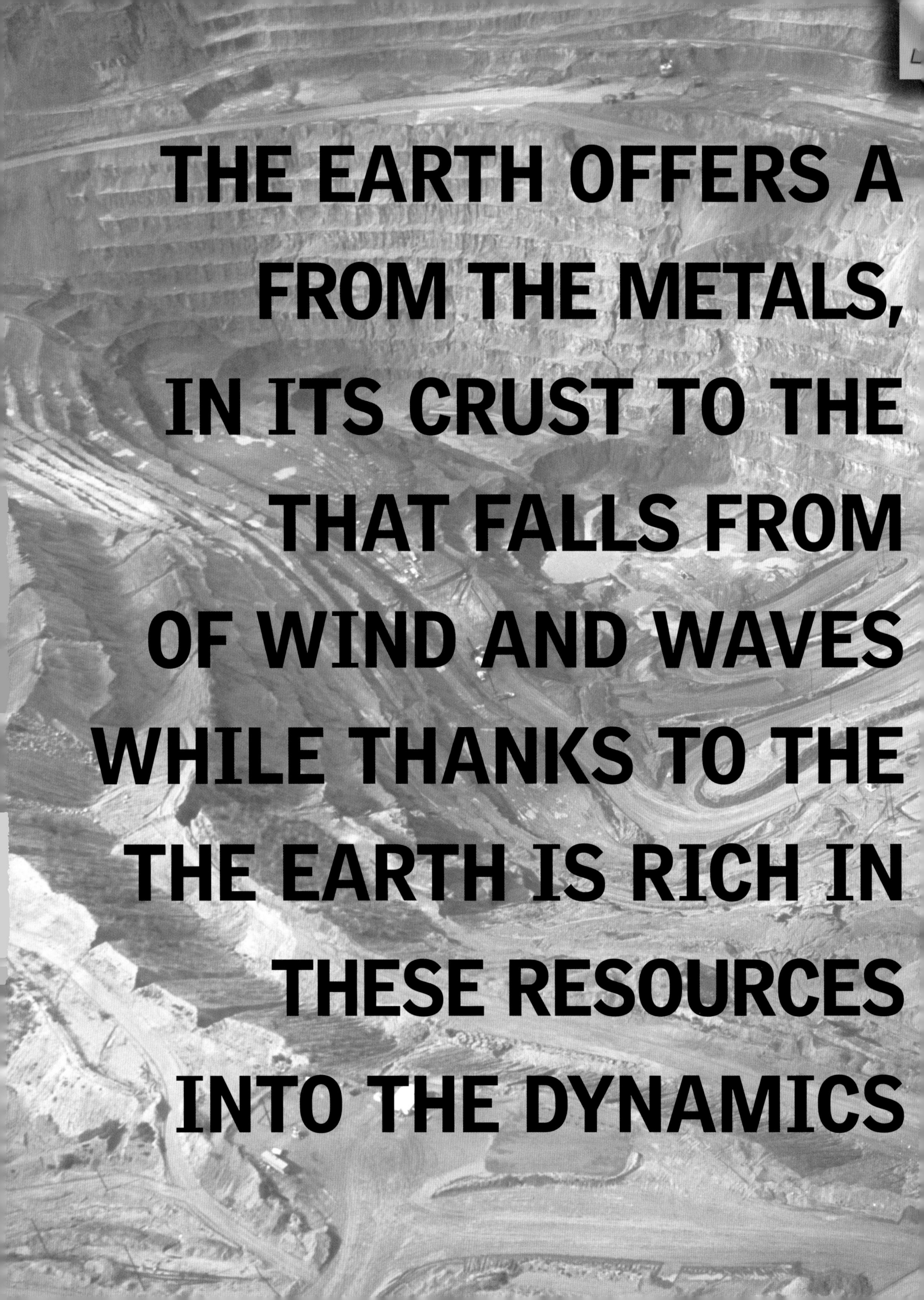

THE EARTH OFFERS A

FROM THE METALS,

IN ITS CRUST TO THE

THAT FALLS FROM

OF WIND AND WAVES

WHILE THANKS TO THE

THE EARTH IS RICH IN

THESE RESOURCES

INTO THE DYNAMICS

TREASURY OF RICHES, GEMS AND MINERALS LIFE-GIVING WATER THE SKY. THE ENERGY CAN GENERATE POWER, SUN'S HEAT AND LIGHT LIFE. UNDERSTANDING GIVES AN INSIGHT OF OUR PLANET.

SALT IN THE DANAKIL DEPRESSION Thick layers of salt deposits spread across the Danakil Depression in Eritrea and Ethiopia, one of the lowest and hottest places on Earth. Lying within East Africa's Great Rift Valley, the depression forms a vast 1000 km² basin, sinking 120 m below sea level in places. Once, the region was part of the Red Sea, but volcanic eruptions separated it from the sea, and the sizzling African sun evaporated the water to leave behind massive salt deposits. Local Afar tribesmen mine the salt, cutting it into thick slabs, which they transport by mule.

DIAMONDS

Indian Ocean

South Africa

DIAMONDS

Oceanic Crust

Volcanic Rock

Continental Crust

SOUTH AFRICAN DIAMONDS
Some of the world's most spectacular diamonds have been found in the Cullinan (formerly Premier) mine, including the Cullinan, Centenary and Golden Jubilee stones. The mine, which lies 25 km north-east of Pretoria, follows the outline of a huge carrot-shaped 'pipe' of kimberlite, the source rock for diamonds – cooled magma from deep in the Earth brought to the surface by ancient volcanic activity. The Cullinan pipe is the largest of a cluster of 12 in the region.

SIBERIAN GAS BONANZA
The world's largest onshore gas field lies beneath Novyy Urengoy in the north-western Siberian Plateau. Since 1977, it has yielded huge supplies – current yearly production is 260 000 million m³ of gas and 825 000 tonnes of oil. As more gas is extracted, the excavations have had to go deeper into the frozen tundra.

GEMS

BURMESE RUBIES Myanmar is renowned for gem-rich gravels, which hold sapphires, peridots and some of the world's finest rubies (left), with an intense red colour described as 'pigeon's blood'. Gemstones tend to be harder and more resistant to weathering than the rock in which they formed. When a gem-bearing rock is eroded, the gems are washed out and deposited downstream in river gravels.

China

GRANITE

Sedimentary Rock

GEMS

Myanmar

Continental Crust

Oceanic Crust

OIL

SAUDI BLACK GOLD Oil and natural gas are always found in what were once ancient sedimentary basins, now buried underground or under the seabed. They formed from the remains of microscopic plankton that fell to the seabed when they died, more than 300 million years ago. Burial, compaction and heating turned the organic material first into crude oil and then into gas. Saudi Arabia (left) and the other Gulf states lie on what was once a huge sedimentary basin, giving them 62 per cent of the world's oil and gas reserves.

SALT

The Gulf

OIL

Red Sea   SALT   Africa

GAS

Russia

GAS

Asia   Siberia

GRANITE

CARVING CHINESE GRANITE A quarry worker shapes blocks of granite building stone. China is the world's leading exporter of dimension stone – stone that has been shaped into blocks. Granite, a type of igneous rock, formed from molten rock that cooled slowly deep within the Earth's crust. This makes it tough and resistant to erosion. Although granite is common all over the world, particular types are specific to certain areas and, depending on the minerals present, they can be pink, grey or black with flecks of other colour. The more attractive granites are used in worktops, building facades and monuments.

EARTH'S RICHES

1 THE SOLAR POWERHOUSE

16 CONSTANT SUN
20 WHAT SUNLIGHT DOES
24 LIGHT AND LIFE
28 PUTTING THE SUN TO WORK

2 ENERGY FROM WITHIN

34 MADE OF STARS
36 FIRE DOWN BELOW
38 DYNAMIC EARTH
42 GEOTHERMAL ENERGY
46 NUCLEAR ENERGY
48 POWER OF THE ATOM

5 RICH AND RARE

94 GOLD
98 LUCKY STRIKES
100 INDUSTRIAL GOLD
102 SMELTING GOLD
104 STOCKPILED GOLD
106 PRECIOUS METALS
110 DIAMONDS
116 NATURE'S TREASURE CHEST

6 STRENGTH TO STRENGTH

122 METAL ORES
126 THE AGE OF ALLOYS
128 METAL FROM SPACE
130 AGE OF IRON
132 STEEL
134 MODERN METALS
138 RECYCLING METALS

3 STORED ENERGY

54 WOOD
56 BIOFUEL
58 COAL AND PEAT
62 OIL
68 NATURAL GAS
72 ENERGY RESOURCES

4 WATER AND WIND POWER

76 WATER AS A RESOURCE
78 THE WATERY PLANET
80 HYDROPOWER
86 TIDAL POWER
88 WAVE POWER
90 WIND POWER

7 UNSUNG RICHES

142 SALT OF THE EARTH
146 STRUCTURAL ROCK
150 THE CONCRETE JUNGLE
152 MATERIAL WORLD

INTRODUCTION

THE EARTH IS A TREASURE CHEST OF RESOURCES – FROM PRECIOUS DIAMONDS AND GOLD, TO THE RAW MATERIALS OF INDUSTRY. There are vast buried energy stores of oil, gas, coal and uranium, and energy can be harnessed from the Sun, water, wind and tides. Some resources took millions of years to form and are limited in their extent, while others are renewable and continually replaced.

As well as the material riches of the Earth, our planet has another form of wealth: **life**. The abundance and range of life on Earth, known as **biodiversity,** is unique to our planet. Already scientists have identified nearly **two million species** and there are millions more besides. From the depths of the ocean to the highest peaks, and from the hottest, driest desert regions to the coldest climes, animals and plants make use of every available habitat and niche. At the bottom of the food chain are the plants and bacteria that fix the energy of the Sun through **photosynthesis**. Higher life forms then feed on these organisms, and in turn become food for other animals.

The Sun plays a vital role in sustaining life on Earth. For 4.6 billion years it has been constantly pouring out energy as light and warmth, making the Earth hospitable for life. As well as powering photosynthesis, the Sun's energy heats

the air, creating wind and waves, which can be used to turn **turbines** and generate **electricity**. The Sun draws water from the Earth's surface, moving it via clouds to precipitate out as rain or snow on higher ground. As this water flows back towards the oceans, we can capture some of its energy via **watermills** and **hydropower plants**. We can even capture the Sun's energy directly using **solar panels** and **photovoltaic cells**.

Many of the Earth's resources were created as a result of the movement of rocks and redistribution of elements, known as the **rock cycle**. Powering this movement is a hot core of liquid metal. The heat that dissipates from the bowels of the Earth creates **convection currents** in the molten rock that moves whole continents, forcing them to crash into each other or pull them apart. Manifestations of this internal heat include hot springs and geysers, whose energy can be tapped to produce geothermal power.

From the **stone** used to make the earliest tools and dwellings to **silicon** – an abundant element with many modern applications, including microchips and contact lenses – man has always drawn from the Earth's bountiful harvest. The challenge that lies ahead is to ensure that these riches are available for many generations to come.

THE SOLAR
POWERHO

USE

1

WE RELY ON THE SUN FOR DAYLIGHT AND MOST OF OUR ENERGY. Usually, we take it for granted, but during a total eclipse we get a taste of how the world would be without the Sun's warmth and light. Stephen Smith from Jedburgh, Scotland, witnessed the 2006 total eclipse in Antalya in southern Turkey. It had been a warm, sunny morning, but that changed as the Moon blocked out the Sun. 'It went dark and there was this really eerie atmosphere. The stars came out and it was the middle of the day – that was the most awesome part about it. It wasn't total darkness, more a sort of deep purplish twilight – and so cold.... People who were wearing T-shirts had to put jumpers on. During totality everything just seemed to stop. The birds stopped singing and traffic on a nearby highway came to a halt as people got out of their cars to look at the sky.'

CONSTANT SUN

THE SUN IS SO LARGE THAT A MILLION EARTHS COULD FIT INSIDE IT. For the last 4.6 billion years, this great ball of gases, mainly hydrogen and helium, has been radiating energy at the rate of 1.4×10^{31} joules an hour, **and it will carry on doing so for another 5 billion years.** To put these figures into perspective, scientists estimate that every day more solar energy falls to Earth than the total amount of energy the planet's current 6 billion inhabitants would consume in 27 years. And that is less than a billionth of the energy that the Sun produces – the rest is lost in space.

This colossal energy production is the result of a process called fusion taking place at the Sun's core. The temperature and density of the gases are so huge in the core that fusion turns hydrogen atoms into helium atoms. When this happens energy is released.

And yet, in terms of the whole Universe, our Sun is pretty average. Compared with other stars, it is not particularly massive or energetic, and at 4.6 billion years old it is roughly middle-aged. This is just as well, because it means that conditions are perfect for life to exist on the Earth. A larger star would burn more brightly and have a shorter lifetime of about 1–2 billion years, not long enough for higher types of life to evolve; a more energetic star would be prone to sudden and large outbursts of radiation, which would destroy life on our planet.

GOLDEN GLOBE The Sun rises in a blaze of glory over Notsuke Bay in Japan (opposite). Here, we are seeing the layer of the Sun called the photosphere. The only times in which we can see the corona and chromosphere are during solar eclipses, when the Moon blocks out the photosphere.

Layers, flares and sunspots

The Sun has several layers. Around the core is the photosphere, the part we see in the sky. Above that are layers called the chromosphere and the corona, which are not normally visible. The photosphere is in constant movement. Massive eruptions occur regularly, producing flares thousands of kilometres long, and dark regions called sunspots move across it. Astronomers believe that both phenomena are a result of changes in the magnetic fields of the photosphere, chromosphere and corona.

Sunspots are regions of intense magnetism, up to 80 000 km across and about 1500°C cooler than the rest of the surface of the Sun. They can last anything from a few hours to several weeks, and their number and position appear to vary in an 11-year cycle. They seem to affect the Earth's climate, although the exact mechanism governing this remains uncertain. Scientists calculate a figure called the solar constant, which is the amount of solar radiation falling on $1\,m^2$ at the edge of Earth's atmosphere. When sunspots are most numerous – the solar maximum – the solar constant rises slightly to 1367 watts/m^2. This phenomenon has been associated with higher global temperatures. During the part of the cycle when sunspot activity is low, known as the solar minimum, the solar constant drops to 1365 watts/m^2, and this has been linked with cooler conditions on Earth. From 1645 to 1715, for example, there was very little sunspot activity, and during this time Europe experienced a prolonged cold spell: in winter the River Thames in London froze over and glaciers advanced in the Alps.

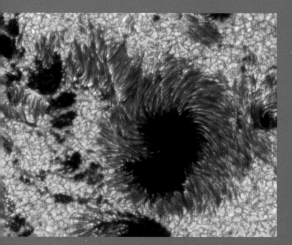

BLACK ON GOLD Sunspots appear as dark blobs encircled with lighter filaments against the surrounding hotter, brighter regions of the photosphere.

DAYS AND SEASONS

THE EARTH IS CONSTANTLY IN MOTION. As you read this, you are travelling on a sphere that is revolving on its axis at a rate of 1600 km/h and moving through space in orbit around the Sun at more than 100 000 km/h. Each revolution takes 24 hours, and it takes roughly 365 days for the Earth to travel around the Sun.

As with all planets in the solar system, the Earth's orbit around the Sun is elliptical. The point where it is closest to the Sun is called the perihelion (meaning 'near the Sun' in Greek), and the point where it is farthest away is called the aphelion ('away from the Sun'). You might think that summer is when the Earth is closest to the Sun and winter when it is farthest away, but this is not the case.

The seasons arise because the Earth is tilted at 23.5 degrees from the vertical. This means that as it moves around the Sun there is a point in its orbit where the North Pole is facing towards the Sun. This occurs on June 21, the longest day in the Northern Hemisphere, called the summer solstice. Six months later the South Pole is facing the Sun. This is the Northern Hemisphere's winter solstice – December 21, the shortest day. The mid points between the solstices, when the lengths of day and night are equal, are called the equinoxes.

Another factor affecting climate and the seasons is the curvature of the Earth, which means that the Sun's heat doesn't

MIDSUMMER SUN The Sun rises over Stonehenge in Wiltshire, England, on Midsummer's Day, the summer solstice. Ancient peoples celebrated the solstices and equinoxes, and they often built stone circles, aligning certain stones with the rising or setting Sun on significant days. Knowing how the days and seasons changed was vital – it told them when to sow and harvest their crops.

fall evenly over the planet. Around the Equator, heat from the Sun has less atmosphere to travel through before reaching land or ocean, which is why the tropics are hotter than the rest of the globe. At the poles the Sun's rays come in at an oblique angle and so must pass through a greater thickness of atmosphere.

Eccentric Earth

The dates of the solstices, equinoxes, aphelion and perihelion are generally considered as fixed, but very slowly they are changing. This is because the Earth's orbit and rotation are not quite constant and change over a long cycle. Although these changes are minuscule each year, they add up over time and account for long-term changes in climate, including the periodic glaciations called ice ages. The Serbian mathematician Milutin Milankovich first put forward the theory that three cycles – the Milankovich cycles – affect the climate on Earth.

The first cycle relates to the Earth's 'eccentricity', or how its orbit around the Sun departs from being a perfect circle. Over

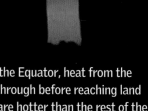

AUTUMN EQUINOX
12 HOURS OF DAYLIGHT

SUMMER
SOLSTICE
15.4 HOURS OF
DAYLIGHT

R
E
OF
T

SPRING EQUINOX
12 HOURS OF DAYLIGHT

HOURS OF DAYLIGHT Day length depends on latitude as well as the time of year. This diagram shows seasonal variation in daylight at 45°North, about the latitude of Bordeaux in France (indicated by the yellow circles). Here, there is a little under 15^1/$_2$ hours of daylight at the summer solstice and a little over 8^1/$_2$ hours at the winter one. Variations are much more extreme in far northern or far southern latitudes. In Longyearbyen in the Norwegian archipelago of Svalbard, residents have six weeks of permanent darkness in midwinter and six weeks of non-stop daylight in midsummer. Around the Equator, daylength varies little: Iquitos in Peru has 12 hours of daylight all year round.

MIDNIGHT SUN Communities such as Longyearbyen, far north of the Arctic Circle in Norway, enjoy permanent sunshine in midsummer. This photograph was taken at midnight.

a timescale of 100 000 years, the orbit changes from almost circular to more elliptical. When the orbit is nearly circular, the Earth is only 3 per cent closer to the Sun at the perihelion than it is at the aphelion; when the orbit is most elliptical, the difference rises to 10–15 per cent, leading to more extreme seasons.

The second cycle relates to the Earth's obliquity, or tilt, which varies between 21.5 and 24.5 degrees from the vertical on a 40 000-year cycle. The change in angle also affects the seasons. When there is less of an axial tilt, the seasons are less distinct because the Sun's energy is more evenly distributed between winter and summer. The current angle is 23.5 degrees.

The final variable is called precession. This is the Earth's slow wobble as it spins on its axis – a good analogy is with a spinning top wobbling as it slows down, although the Earth is not slowing down. Over 23 000 years, the Earth's axis moves round in a circle, and this affects whether the aphelion and perihelion occur in winter or summer. When the perihelion falls in the Northern Hemisphere's winter, as it does at present, the Earth's relative closeness to the Sun moderates the severity of the winter. In about 10 000 years' time, this will be reversed. The perihelion will coincide with the Northern Hemisphere's summer solstice, bringing hotter summers and greater seasonal contrasts.

WHAT SUNLIGHT DOES

AS WELL AS LIGHTING OUR DAYS, the Sun's energy helps to keep the Earth at a temperature where a vast variety of life can flourish. Clouds reflect a significant proportion of the energy in sunlight straight back out to space, but the remainder heats the oceans, the land and the atmosphere. The heated air and evaporated water create the weather systems, while plants capture the energy to make sugars. In the process, plants absorb carbon dioxide and release oxygen and so maintain conditions in the atmosphere that are favourable to life.

Some of the world's most dramatic landscapes are the result of weathering, itself a result of the movement of wind, heat and rain across the Earth, driven by the energy in sunlight.

Reflectance and Earthshine

Sunlight travels as a wave of vibrating and magnetic fields, collectively termed the electromagnetic spectrum. Most sunlight reaching our atmosphere is within the visible range, with wavelengths of between 400 and 700 nanometres – a nanometre (nm) is one-thousand-millionth of a metre. But sunlight also includes an infrared component (with wavelengths greater than 700 nm) and some ultraviolet (less than 400 nm).

The amount of light an object reflects is called its albedo, and it is usually measured as a fraction. As a whole, the Earth reflects about 30 per cent of sunlight back into space, so its average albedo is expressed as 0.3. But different surfaces reflect different amounts of light, and as a result the albedo varies significantly over the surface of the Earth, depending on geographical location and time of year. Clouds reflect a lot of sunlight – they have very high albedos, usually higher than the surfaces beneath them. Deserts also have high albedos, as does snow cover. Oceans, by contrast, have low albedos. Scientists combine the measurement of the Earth's average albedo with a measure of the solar constant (see page 18) so that they can estimate the energy input to the planet.

WEATHERED MAJESTY Famous from many a movie Western, Monument Valley in southern Utah, USA, is a product of weathering and erosion. The rusty red of the landscape is the result of air oxidising iron in the rock.

One way to see the effect of the Earth's albedo is to get up before dawn on a spring day when there is a New Moon. Take a look at the crescent Moon and you may just be able to see the 'dark' part of the Moon faintly glowing. You are looking at Earthshine, the result of sunlight bouncing off the Earth and being reflected in its turn by the Moon. Leonardo da Vinci first recorded the phenomenon in the 16th century. Today, scientists measure it to help them to work out the amount of sunlight being reflected from the Earth – a key factor when attempting to calculate global warming and climate change.

EARTHSHINE *Sunlight reflected from the Earth illuminates the dark part of a New Moon, sometimes called the 'old Moon in the New Moon's arms'.*

more vapour. As the warm air moves upwards, it expands and cools down. As it cools, it is less able to hold water vapour, and the excess is forced out as droplets that form clouds or rain. From fluffy white cumulus to towering thunderclouds, the basic cloud-forming process is the same.

Another factor in global weather systems is the way that more heat from the Sun hits the equatorial regions. Warm air rising from the Equator moves outwards and upwards towards the poles and is replaced beneath by surface winds moving towards the Equator. These winds are called trade winds. Due to the rotation of the Earth, the trade winds blow from the south-east in the Southern Hemisphere and from the north-east in the Northern Hemisphere.

WEATHER SYSTEMS

ANY SUNLIGHT NOT IMMEDIATELY REFLECTED BACK OUT TO SPACE IS HELD IN THE ATMOSPHERE. Its infrared component (as well as heat radiated from the ground) heats air up, and as it does so, the air expands. Being more buoyant than the cooler air around it, the hot air moves upwards. When it reaches higher levels in the atmosphere the air cools down and it begins to descend. This circulating flow is the basis for most weather systems and is called convection.

When sunlight hits the oceans, it evaporates water. The humid air rises in much the same way as heated air, pulling the water vapour into the upper atmosphere. The amount of vapour held in the air depends on temperature – warmer air carries

Shaping landscapes

Some of the world's most dramatic landscapes are the result of weathering, itself a result of the movement of wind, heat and rain across the Earth, driven by the energy in sunlight. Weathering may be physical, chemical or biological. Changes in temperature or pressure cause physical weathering, mostly in Arctic and mountainous regions. If water gets into fissures in a rock, it expands as it freezes, exerting pressure on the rock. Successive freeze-thaw cycles mean that the rock eventually fractures.

A similar process, called insolation weathering, occurs in deserts, where temperatures soar in the day and plummet at night. In some deserts, the temperature difference may be 30°C.

*REFRACTED BEAUTY Sunlight refracted and
reflected by raindrops creates the perfect arc of
a rainbow over the coast of Irian Jaya, Indonesia.*

Over time, the continual expansion and shrinking of the rock
surface creates stresses between the layers of rock, eventually
causing fracturing or shattering. Bryce Canyon in southern Utah,
USA, is a striking example of such processes. Jagged pinnacles of
crumbling rock appear like a city of decaying minarets as
limestone gives way to the elements.

Physical weathering predisposes the rock for the second
kind of weathering, chemical weathering, which is a reaction
between the rock and air, water or other solutions. When rain
combines with carbon dioxide in the air, it forms a weakly acidic
solution. The solution can dissolve certain minerals, such as
calcium carbonate, the main component of limestone. Over time,
the passage of acidic water can carve out huge underground
caverns in limestone. Sometimes, the dissolved limestone is
redeposited elsewhere as stalactites and stalagmites. Water also
reacts with minerals in the rock, such as feldspars (a type of
silicate), and breaks them down.

Another type of chemical weathering, salt weathering,
occurs on coastal rocks where seawater splashes against the
rock and then evaporates, leaving salt crystals behind. As the salt
crystals form, they expand, pushing surface layers apart and

producing pockmarks in the surface of the rock. The air may also
oxidise minerals within the rock, such as iron in ironstone, which
'rusts' on exposed surfaces.

The third type of weathering is caused by biological agents.
Bacteria and lichens obtain nutrients from the surface of rocks
by using acids to dissolve minerals within them, which they then
absorb. Plants can also cause damage when their roots invade the
joints of rocks and force them apart. This can be seen in urban
areas, where tree roots penetrate and crack pavements and roads.

Greenhouse effect

About half of the sunlight that enters the atmosphere and passes
through the clouds reaches the surface of the Earth, where it is
absorbed and radiated upwards in the form of heat. Most of this
infrared heat (90 per cent of it) is absorbed by 'greenhouse'
gases in the atmosphere – including carbon dioxide, water
vapour, methane, nitrous oxides and chlorofluorocarbons – and
radiated back down towards the Earth again. This trapping of
heat in the atmosphere is called the greenhouse effect. It is
important because without it the atmosphere on Earth would be
30–40°C cooler – too cold to sustain life.

But scientists believe that human activity is magnifying
the greenhouse effect, mainly due to emissions of carbon dioxide
from burning fossil fuels. There is evidence that the Earth's
average surface air temperature has increased globally by 0.5°C

since 1850. The three warmest years on record have all occurred since 1998. In 2007, a report by the Intergovernmental Panel on Climate Change stated that there was a 90 per cent certainty that the burning of fossil fuels and other human activities are changing the Earth's climate.

The consequences of an increased greenhouse effect, known as global warming, are widespread and difficult to predict. It is likely that oceans will expand as they are warmed and icecaps will melt, both of which will raise the sea level. Some regions will become warmer, and weather patterns will be disrupted. Vegetation and crops will be affected by changes in climate. Scientists fear that there may also be feedback mechanisms that will accelerate the warming further.

OPTICAL EFFECTS

HAVE YOU EVER WONDERED WHY A CLOUDLESS SKY IS BLUE? The answer lies in the way light travels and the fact that shorter wavelength light is scattered more than longer wavelengths. Sunlight is actually a combination of colours and each colour has a different wavelength and frequency. Light travels in straight lines through the vacuum of space, but when it reaches Earth it bumps into molecules in the atmosphere and scatters.

Visible light is composed of wavelengths ranging from 400 nm (violet) to 700 nm (red light), with the rest of the colours of the rainbow in between. The atmosphere is mainly composed of oxygen and nitrogen molecules, which are much smaller than the wavelength of light. When light hits one of these molecules it is deflected from its straight path and scattered. Light of shorter wavelengths, in the violet and blue range, is scattered the most, so the sky appears blue.

Other interesting and beautiful optical phenomena occur in the atmosphere when light is refracted or reflected off water droplets or ice crystals. The most familiar is a rainbow, the result of the refraction and reflection of sunlight as it shines through a shower of rain. Each raindrop acts like a prism, bending the sunlight, or refracting it, into the different colours from red to violet. The backs of the spherical raindrops then reflect the light, much like a curved mirror would, creating the classic rainbow arc across the sky.

Mirages

Every summer a ghostly city, with several buildings and a church, appears on the Mount Fairweather Glacier on the border between Alaska and Canada. People call it the Silent City of Alaska. It is, in fact, a mirage. Some people have even identified the buildings as standing in Bristol, around 14 000 km away.

Mirages often occur in regions of extreme cold, as in Alaska, or extreme heat, as in the Sahara. Sailors in cold waters have been convinced that they have seen ships 'floating' in the sky, while travellers in the desert may spot a shimmering far-off oasis, only to find that it never existed. These mirages occur because the air separates into two layers of different densities, affecting the way that light is refracted through it. In the desert, a layer of very hot air forms over the sandy surface. Rays of light from an object beyond the horizon are refracted as they travel through this region so they appear parallel to the ground. The object looks as though it is in a shimmering pool of water. In cold regions, such as around the Arctic Circle, the air closest to the ground is colder than that above it. This refracts light from objects over the horizon so they appear suspended in the sky.

WATER TRICK These zebras in Namibia look as if they are walking through water. In fact, the water is an optical illusion – a heat mirage.

LIGHT AND LIFE

PERHAPS THE MOST STRIKING ASPECT OF OUR PLANET IS ITS ABUNDANCE OF LIFE. From the ocean depths to the mountain tops, all manner of animals and plants live on the Earth. They make use of every available habitat and niche and are all connected in huge and complex ecosystems. This sheer variety of life is called biodiversity, and it appears to be a unique feature of the Earth. Although astronomers have searched long and hard, so far they have failed to find any form of life in outer space – let alone the multitude of species we are used to seeing on our planet.

Capturing sunlight

Most of this life would not be able to exist without the energy of the Sun, fixed through the process called photosynthesis. Every day, billions of plants and bacteria, from the tallest trees in the tropical rainforests to microscopic phytobacteria drifting through the oceans, tune in to the Sun's energy. Through photosynthesis, they turn it into stored energy, absorb carbon dioxide and release oxygen.

Arguably the most important chemical reaction on Earth, photosynthesis captures less than 1 per cent of the Sun's energy, yet this 1 per cent provides all our food and much of our fuel – fossil fuels were derived from sunlight millions of years ago. What, then, is it? The reaction is a complicated one, usually summarised as:

$$6CO_2 + 6H_2O + sunlight \longrightarrow C_6H_{12}O_6 + 6O_2$$
$$carbon\ dioxide + water + sunlight \longrightarrow glucose + oxygen$$

Essentially, photosynthetic organisms use sunlight to convert carbon dioxide and water into glucose (a type of sugar), releasing oxygen as a byproduct. The glucose, a stored form of energy, is then turned into more complicated chemicals and forms the basis of all foodchains, while oxygen is a major component of the air we breathe.

OCEAN DIVERSITY The highest biodiversity in the oceans is found in coral reefs. Even though they usually occur in nutrient-poor waters, efficient recycling of nutrients allows a huge range of fish and other species to thrive.

GREEN LEAVES In plant leaves (here, a rose leaf), a pigment called chlorophyll captures the energy from sunlight. It absorbs light in the blue and red parts of the spectrum and so reflects green light.

DIVERSITY UNDER THREAT

SO FAR SCIENTISTS HAVE IDENTIFIED ALMOST 2 MILLION SPECIES OF PLANTS AND ANIMALS, BUT THIS IS ONLY A FRACTION OF THE NUMBER THAT HAVE YET TO BE IDENTIFIED. Estimates for the total number of life forms on the planet range anywhere between 5 and 100 million. This includes species that have barely been studied, from microscopic organisms, such as viruses and bacteria, to mysterious creatures living in the darkest depths of the ocean or under the icecaps.

Biodiversity is not only precious in itself, but also vital to our survival as a species. As the human population expands – currently more than 6 billion people – we have an increasing impact upon other creatures, competing with them for space and resources. Yet it is in our interests to preserve them. Plants and animals are a key source of new materials, food and medicine. We use many plants in the pharmaceutical industry, and we can only imagine what other useful compounds will be produced from as yet unidentified species. Biodiversity also governs how ecosystems operate, often in complex ways that biologists are only beginning to understand. Water cycling, soil formation, pollination of plants and regulation of climate are just some of the systems that depend on a diverse array of different life forms.

HOT SPOT Biodiversity does not occur equally over the planet. Lobelias and greenswords are among an exceptional diversity of species that flourish on Hawaii's Maui island.

But there is evidence that biodiversity is under threat – we are currently losing species at an unprecedented rate. According to the UN's Millennium Ecosystem Assessment in 2005, changes in biodiversity have been more rapid in the past 50 years than at any time in human history, and the current extinction rate is at least 100 times faster than the natural evolutionary rate. We are in the middle of a mass extinction, unparalleled since the catastrophic impact that wiped out the dinosaurs 65 million years ago.

Habitat loss
The biggest reason is the destruction of habitat worldwide, often to make way for crops and livestock. Some modern farming methods destroy diversity by growing a single species or handful of species to the exclusion of others and the indiscriminate use of pesticides. Habitat is also destroyed by construction projects, such as dams, roads and settlements.

The second largest threat to rare species is exotic invaders, invasive species that humans have introduced to new areas. These often compete with native species for food and habitat. One example is the grey squirrel, which has virtually replaced the native red squirrel in the UK. Originally from North America, the grey squirrel was introduced in the late 19th century and quickly took over from the red squirrel, because it is more adaptable in its diet and habitat. Today, red squirrels exist in a few isolated regions, while the grey squirrel is widespread and numerous.

Another factor is hunting, which has led to the extinction of many species and put several others on the endangered list. Despite the UN Convention on International Trade in Endangered Species, which was set up in 1975 to control the trade in protected animals, poaching of animals, such as the big cats and elephants, remains a problem.

CHLOROPHYLL DENSITY
Most plants and some phytoplankton in the oceans use the green pigment chlorophyll to absorb the energy in sunlight. Other photosynthetic organisms contain red, blue or brown pigments, called phycobilins, or pigments that absorb infrared light. The satellite images (below) show the density of organisms with chlorophyll across the globe. The range is from dark green (most dense) to yellow (least dense) on land, and from red (most dense) to pink (least dense) in the oceans.

ARCTIC AND NORTHERN HEMISPHERE

ANTARCTIC AND SOUTHERN HEMISPHERE

What can be done?
International efforts are being made to save the Earth's diversity of species. In 1992, the nations meeting at the Earth Summit in Rio de Janeiro agreed a treaty called the Convention on Biological Diversity, which came into force the next year. In 2003, all signed-up countries agreed to achieve a 'significant reduction of the current rate of biodiversity loss at the global, regional and national level as a contribution to poverty alleviation and to the benefit of all life on Earth'. The Swiss-based World Conservation Union, meanwhile, encourages conservation efforts worldwide, publishing a Red List of Threatened Species, which describes endangered species.

In 2007, the Zoological Society of London (ZSL) launched its own EDGE (Evolutionarily Distinct and Globally Endangered) campaign to focus world attention on unusual animals that are currently both endangered and have few close relatives. The ZSL looked at every known mammal species on Earth and gave each one a score based on how genetically distinct and how endangered it is. They ended up with 100 species of the world's most unusual creatures that are currently under threat. They include the Yangtze river dolphin from China, which may already be extinct; the long-beaked echidna, a primitive mammal from New Guinea that lays eggs like a reptile; and the riverine rabbit from South Africa's Karoo desert, an ancient and rare rabbit species, the sole member of its genus. If these creatures are allowed to become extinct they will be lost forever.

IN 1935, THE CANE TOAD WAS INTRODUCED TO AUSTRALIA
to try to control the cane beetle, a pest of sugar cane. It soon became a pest itself. Much hardier than native frogs, it is a voracious predator, whose tadpoles are poisonous – but it is ineffective against cane beetles. It is now found through most of Queensland and parts of the Northern Territory.

EVERY YEAR some 20,000 km² of Amazonian rainforest are cleared. On a global scale, 130,000 km² of forest are lost annually.

A SPECIES IS LOST FOR EVER
SOMEWHERE in the world every 20 minutes, according to some experts.

FACTS

PUTTING THE SUN TO WORK

STAND IN THE SUNSHINE, AND YOU APPRECIATE THE EFFECTS OF SOLAR THERMAL ENERGY AS IT WARMS YOUR SKIN. People have used this sort of 'passive' solar heating for thousands of years. In prehistoric times, they made their homes in caves in south-facing cliff walls, because they knew that these would be warmer than north-facing ones, and gardeners have long known about the heating effects of greenhouses. Nowadays, sunshine is an increasingly important, pollution-free source of power, thanks to advances in technology, which enable us to capture its energy more efficiently. This is done in three ways: by solar thermal collectors, by photovoltaic cells (see box, opposite) and by concentrating solar power plants or furnaces.

PASSIVE HEATING Marine iguanas on the Galápagos Islands bask in the Sun. As cold-blooded animals, they need the Sun's heat to revitalise them after a cold dive in the Pacific.

Passive or active collection

Thermal collectors can be passive or active. Passive ones include design features such as 'sunspaces', which work rather like greenhouses. A building is constructed with a south-facing, glazed area. This heats up in the Sun, and ventilation systems then circulate the heated air to other parts of the building. Another such feature is a Trombe wall (named after the French engineer and solar heating pioneer, Félix Trombe): a south-facing wall, usually painted black to absorb the most heat. The wall heats up slowly during the day and gives out heat during the night as it cools.

Active systems convert solar energy into heat, which can be transported for use elsewhere. Again, the principle behind them has been known for centuries – that the Sun heats up water in a dark vessel. In the most common system, a flat-plate absorber intercepts and absorbs sunlight. It has a transparent cover, usually glass, which allows solar energy through while reducing heat loss, and a heat-insulating backing. A fluid, often water, flows through copper pipes, removing the heat from the absorber to a storage tank. For the greatest efficiency, a fixed flat-plate collector is mounted on a south-facing, sloping roof in good sunlight.

Concentrating solar power

Active thermal collectors are most often used on a small scale, for domestic water heating or heating swimming pools. Solar power plants work on a far larger scale, producing electricity in much the same way as conventional power stations, but by harnessing the Sun's energy, rather than nuclear power or coal. Sunshine is used to heat air or a fluid, which is pumped through heat exchangers to produce superheated steam. This is then fed to a steam turbine to generate electricity. Because of the high temperatures needed, these plants have concentrators, usually mirrors, to focus the solar energy on a single point. The three main types are parabolic troughs, solar dishes and solar towers.

In a parabolic trough, a series of trough-shaped mirrors concentrates sunlight onto tubes carrying a fluid such as oil, located at the trough's focal line. The fluid absorbs the

PHOTOVOLTAIC CELLS

Solar or photovoltaic (PV) cells – the kind used in calculators – convert sunlight directly into electricity. They are made of thin layers of semi-conducting material, such as silicon. When light shines on them, they create an electric field across the layers, causing an electric current to flow. The cells can be connected in modules of up to 50 and fitted on the roofs of houses, as here in Japan. They do not need direct sunlight to be effective and can be quickly installed. They are often used in remote areas with no conventional electricity supply.

CENTRAL FOCUS Mirrors concentrate the Sun's rays onto a central tower at the solar power plant at Sanlúcar la Mayor in Spain. A steam turbine in the tower drives a generator, which produces electricity.

ODEILLO

THE MOST POWERFUL SOLAR FURNACE

IN THE WORLD WAS COMPLETED IN 1970 IN THE FRENCH SKI RESORT OF ODEILLO. France's National Centre for Scientific Research designed it not to generate electricity, but to create incredibly high temperatures for use in experiments. Under the clear skies of the Pyrenees, with 300 days of sunshine a year, Odeillo is the perfect location for a complex arrangement of mirrors that concentrate sunlight to a maximum of 3800°C – more than half the temperature on the surface of the Sun.

It works through the use of 63 flat-surfaced mirrors, called heliostats, positioned on eight terraces in front of a huge parabolic focusing mirror, 40 m high and 54 m wide. These smaller mirrors, facing south, automatically track the Sun through the sky, sending the energy in parallel rays onto the parabolic mirror, which focuses the energy into a receptor positioned at its focal point. Here, the Sun's rays are concentrated on an area just 30 cm across. The parabolic mirror is made up of 9000 reflectors, which can be controlled separately, allowing a range of temperatures to be achieved.

Experiments carried out at Odeillo include testing the ceramics used to protect spacecraft as they re-enter the atmosphere, 'cracking' water into hydrogen and oxygen and the synthesis of new materials, such as carbon nanotubes, which are twice as light as aluminium, 100 000 times thinner than a human hair and with a higher conductivity than copper.

POWER OUTPUT 10 kW–1 MW
TEMPERATURES ACHIEVED 800°–3800°C
FOCAL POINT 13 m above ground, 18 m from the surface of the parabolic mirror
LOCATION Commune of Font-Romeu-Odeillo-Via, Pyrénées-Orientales. Open to the public all year.

concentrated radiation, transferring it into thermal energy used to power turbines and produce electricity. Each collector tracks the Sun along an east-west axis during the day to ensure optimum heating. The parabolic shape of its mirror concentrates the sunlight at 30–100 times its normal intensity, so that the fluid can reach temperatures of over 400°C. There are whole 'fields' of collectors, which are often very large, composed of hundreds of parallel rows of single-axis tracking collectors.

The world's largest solar power facility, at Kramer Junction in California, uses parabolic trough technology. It has five solar electric generating stations with a combined capacity of 150 MW. The facility covers more than 400 hectares, and at full capacity it can supply enough power for about 150 000 homes.

SOLAR COOKING Villagers in Assam, India, save on firewood by using a solar cooker. The dish focuses the Sun's rays onto the cooking pot.

SUN RADIO Even in the remotest areas, people can tune in with radios like this, powered by PV cells or a wind-up handle.

In a solar tower, a circular array of mirrors focuses the Sun's energy onto a central receiver at the top of a tower. Europe's first commercial solar power plant uses this technology – Planta Solar 10 (PS10), which began operating at Sanlúcar la Mayor, near Seville in Spain, in March 2007. It uses 624 large heliostat mirrors arranged around a central receiver at the top of a 115 m tower, which generates temperatures of 250°C. The plant has a peak capacity of 11 megawatts and can power 6000 homes.

In a solar dish, a dish-shaped reflector focuses sunlight onto a receiver at its focal point. With this technology, the concentration ratio is much higher than with the other two; the fluid or gas can reach a temperature of 750°C. The solar dish is also more portable and easier to install than a tower or parabolic trough system, which makes it useful for remote locations.

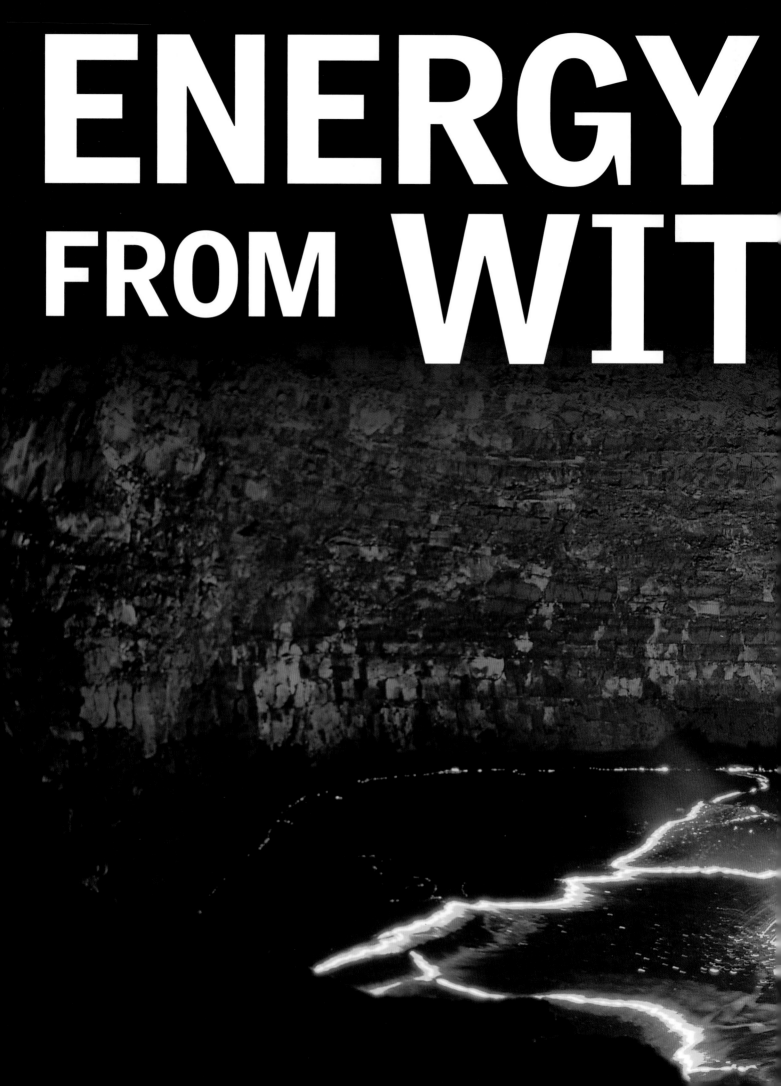

HIN 2

AT THE SUMMIT OF ERTA ALE (DEVIL'S MOUNTAIN) IN ETHIOPIA, GEOLOGISTS ARE GIVEN A TASTE OF WHAT IT IS LIKE DEEP INSIDE THE EARTH. Erta Ale's seething lake of lava has been bubbling at 1000°C for the past 100 years. The Earth's core is thought to be five times as hot. Even the heat near to the surface is so intense that it can move continents, slowly but continuously changing the face of the planet. This activity sorts and mixes the elements, such as silicon, gold and uranium, that were incorporated into the planet at its formation. Some of the internal heat is trapped in underground reservoirs of steam and hot water that provide valuable sources of energy. Scientists are also discovering how to control and use nuclear fusion, the powerful process that created the elements as galaxies and stars formed and died.

MADE OF STARS

ALL THE BRILLIANT GEMS, PRECIOUS METALS, ORGANIC COMPOUNDS (SUCH AS OIL AND COAL), AND MINERALS THAT LIE BURIED DEEP BENEATH THE EARTH'S SURFACE have formed over billions of years from chemical elements that were first forged in the hearts of ancient stars. These elements are the basic building blocks of all matter. In the early Universe, subatomic particles combined to create protons, neutrons and electrons – the three components of atoms. The first atoms to appear were hydrogen and helium, the simplest elements, and clouds of these gases condensed to make the first stars. All elements heavier than hydrogen and helium form only in the immense temperatures and pressures found in stars. Most occur in normal-sized stars, up to one and a half times the mass of our Sun, but the heaviest, such as lead and uranium, form only when massive stars explode into supernovae.

The process by which the nuclei of atoms fuse together to make heavier elements is called nucleosynthesis. Stars the size of the Sun turn hydrogen into helium, releasing huge amounts of energy as they do so. Once the hydrogen has been exhausted, the remaining core is hot enough for helium to fuse into carbon. Then the carbon atoms fuse into heavier elements, such as oxygen, neon and silicon. Eventually, iron is produced. But at this point fusion cannot continue because it would require energy to be taken in rather than given out. The star dies, and the outer layers drift off into space. When a massive star (one at least three times the mass of our Sun) reaches the point when all the hydrogen in its core is used up, it collapses and explodes into a supernova. The energy of this explosion fuels further nuclear fusion, producing heavier elements such as lead and uranium. Clouds of gas and dust containing the newly formed elements drift away. As areas in these clouds cool and collapse, the matter within them gradually condenses to form new galaxies and solar systems.

Rich ingredients

The first stars and galaxies are believed to have appeared about 12 billion years ago. By the time our Solar System began forming 4.6 billion years ago, millions of stars had burnt out, leaving clouds of interstellar dust and gases containing a rich mix of elements. As the cloud from which the Solar System formed began to spin, matter was drawn towards the centre. There, the temperature and pressure increased steadily to the point when hydrogen began to fuse into helium, and the Sun began to release energy. The remaining dust and gases continued to circle the Sun, gradually clumping together, in a process called accretion, to form ever-larger bodies that became the planets. Of the 118 elements so far identified, more than 90 occur naturally on Earth and all of them have been detected in the Universe at large. They include iron, uranium, copper, gold, nitrogen, silicon, neon and carbon – the building block of life itself.

STELLAR FORGE When a massive star collapses and burns helium in its core, nuclear reactions create heavier elements in the surrounding gas shell.

FIRE DOWN BELOW

FOR THE MOST PART THE GROUND WE WALK ON SEEMS COOL AND INERT, YET DEEP BELOW OUR FEET A MASS OF HOT, SOFT ROCK IS CONSTANTLY ON THE MOVE, kept that way by the intense heat generated within the planet. The greater the depth, the greater the heat. Down to about 8 km, the temperature increases by 2–3 degrees every 100 m, while the core temperature is estimated to be about 5000°C. Scientists have measured the temperature in deep mines and boreholes and calculated that the Earth is generating 30-45 terawatts (30-45 trillion watts) of heat from within.

The Earth's layers

The matter that originally formed the Earth included metal-rich fragments, rocky meteorites and icy particles from comets. Heat within the Earth kept these components churning around in a hot, seething mass, and over time denser elements such as iron sank towards the centre, while lighter elements such as silicon and oxygen rose towards the surface, forming the rocky outer layers. As the Earth cooled, three distinct layers formed: the crust, mantle and core.

The outer crust, or lithosphere, is a relatively thin layer of solid, brittle rock. The layer below the crust, called the mantle, contains a greater proportion of iron and magnesium than the crust, so is denser. At the upper edge of the mantle is a layer of partially molten rock called the asthenosphere. The rock in this region is hot enough to flow slowly, and it folds, stretches and compresses without fracturing. The lighter lithosphere floats on the moving asthenosphere. Beneath the mantle is an iron-nickel core comprising a liquid outer core and a solid inner core.

RADIOACTIVE DECAY AND FRICTION GENERATE TEMPERATURES OF 700–1800°C IN THE MANTLE

HEAT IS TRANSFERRED OUTWARDS TOWARDS THE CRUST

HOT, METAL-RICH CORE IS AROUND 5000°C

COOL MATERIAL SINKS BACK INTO THE MANTLE

NORTHERN CALIFORNIA

EARTH'S CRUST AND CONVECTION CURRENTS
Heat is transferred outwards through the mantle to the crust by convection, creating currents in the mantle that keep the molten rock there constantly on the move. This movement in the mantle propels the sections of the crust, or plates, endlessly around the planet's surface, where they slowly collide and push past each other or drift apart.

In northern California, the Pacific and North American plates are grinding past each other. The resulting fault line creates an obvious gash, the San Andreas Fault, in the Earth's surface. The difference in the terrain on either side shows how the two plates have moved over the centuries.

SAN ANDREAS
FAULT

processes produced much more heat in the early Earth than they do now. Elements such as uranium, thorium and potassium in the mantle and crust are unstable and break down over time, giving off heat as they do so. This radioactive decay is currently the source of roughly half the Earth's heat.

A fractured surface

In the early 20th century, the German meteorologist Alfred Wegener tried to account for the jigsaw-like pattern of the continents. He proposed that they were once joined in a huge landmass, which he called Pangaea, and that over millions of years they had drifted apart to their present positions. He also suggested that they were still moving. His theory was greeted with derision by the geological fraternity at the time, and it was not until 30 years after his death that scientists acknowledged he had been right.

Wegener's theory foundered when first proposed because he couldn't explain how the continents moved. Today, we know that their movement is caused by the heat radiating out from Earth's interior. We also know the rate of the movement – around 2.5–15 cm a year – and that this is causing the mountain ranges along their edges, such as the Himalayas, to grow around 1 cm per year.

The lithosphere, or outer crust, varies in thickness from about 5 km under the oceans to 100 km under mountain ranges. It is not a continuous sheet of rock; it is broken into numerous interlocking pieces, known as plates. There are seven major plates – the North American, South American, African, Antarctic, Eurasian, Australian and Pacific – plus a number of smaller ones.

Floating on the asthenosphere, and moved by convection currents as heat dissipates through the mantle, adjacent plates are constantly colliding or drifting apart. This movement accounts for the way in which many surface features are formed – such as the uplifting of mountain ranges where plates push together, rift valleys and deep ocean trenches where they move apart – and for the cataclysmic events, such as earthquakes and volcanoes, that occur along their boundaries. Where plates converge, one slides beneath the other and sinks into the mantle, where it is reassimilated into the molten rock there. All this activity is constantly sorting, shifting and transforming not just the surface of the planet, but the elements within it.

Heat machine

The planet's internal heat is generally thought to come from the decay of radioactive elements, such as uranium, thorium and potassium, distributed throughout its interior, combined with heat from gravitational forces left over from the Earth's formation. Scientists still debate the precise ratios contributed by each of these processes.

The planet grew as a result of collisions between particles and lumps of matter within the forming Solar System. As the particles were moving at speeds of 30 000–50 000 km/h, the collisions created massive amounts of heat energy that became trapped within the Earth. As the Earth grew so did the gravitional force exerted from the centre, causing the planet to compact and shrink, and gravitational energy was converted into heat. These

Intense heat is generated within the planet. Down to about 8 km, the temperature increases by 2–3 degrees every 100 m. Scientists have measured the temperature in deep mines and boreholes and calculated that the Earth is generating 30–45 terawatts (30–45 trillion watts) of heat from within.

DYNAMIC EARTH

IGNEOUS ROCK Most lava flows contain basalt. The geometric pattern of this columnar basalt in Canada occurred because of the way the rock contracted as it cooled.

THE ROCK CYCLE – AN ONGOING PROCESS Rocks at the surface are broken down by rain, frost, ice and wind into smaller fragments. Different types of rock erode into different materials: for example, igneous rocks break down into clays and sands. These are transported by wind, water or ice and deposited as sediments in lakes, rivers, deserts and on the seabed. The sediments are buried by later deposits, eventually compacting into sedimentary rocks, such as sandstone or mudstone. This rock may be buried for millions of years, and if it undergoes extreme heating or is exposed to great pressures, it may be recrystallised into metamorphic rock. All three types can be buried deep enough to melt back into magma. If the magma comes near the surface, it may cool and crystallise into more igneous rock.

TECTONIC ACTIVITY As magma nears the Earth's surface it cools, forming igneous rock. Slow cooling forms intrusive rock (e.g. granite); rapid cooling forms extrusive rock (e.g. basalt).

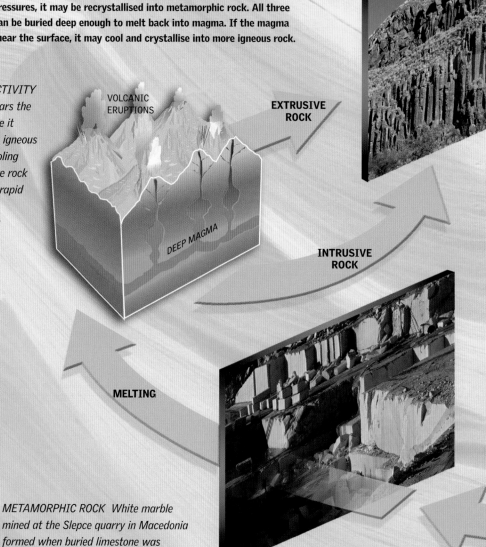

VOLCANIC ERUPTIONS

EXTRUSIVE ROCK

DEEP MAGMA

HEAT AND PRESSURE

INTRUSIVE ROCK

MELTING

HEAT AND PRESSURE

METAMORPHIC ROCK White marble mined at the Slepce quarry in Macedonia formed when buried limestone was subjected to intense heat and pressure.

FORCES OF DESTRUCTION AND RENEWAL ARE CONSTANTLY AT WORK, SHAPING AND SHIFTING THE EARTH'S SURFACE AND THE MATTER WITHIN IT. Molten rock is pushed up to form mountains, which are eroded, and the resulting sediments are carried or washed away, to end up on the seabed. The sediments become compacted into bedrock, which is eventually forced up to the surface by volcanic activity, and the cycle starts again. The whole process is known as the rock cycle (below). It requires stupendous forces working over vast periods of time, and is driven by the Earth's internal heat. The high temperatures and great pressure below ground also trigger the chemical reactions that create different types of rock. This constant transformation and recycling produces the variety of rocks, ores, precious stones and minerals that make up the Earth's riches.

The three types of rock

Igneous rocks crystallise from molten rock, either slowly when magma near the surface cools, or rapidly when lava is thrust to the surface in a volcanic eruption. The molten material crystallises into different rocks, such as granite, basalt and obsidian, depending on its mineral or chemical composition and the speed at which it cools.

Sedimentary rocks form through the process of erosion and deposition in lakes, seas and deserts. Sandstone, limestone, mudstone and conglomerate are all forms of sedimentary rock.

Metamorphic rocks form when buried sedimentary or igneous rocks are subjected to such high heat and pressure that the atoms within the grains of rock re-combine with each other to form new substances. Limestone can be metamorphosed into marble, and mudstone into slate.

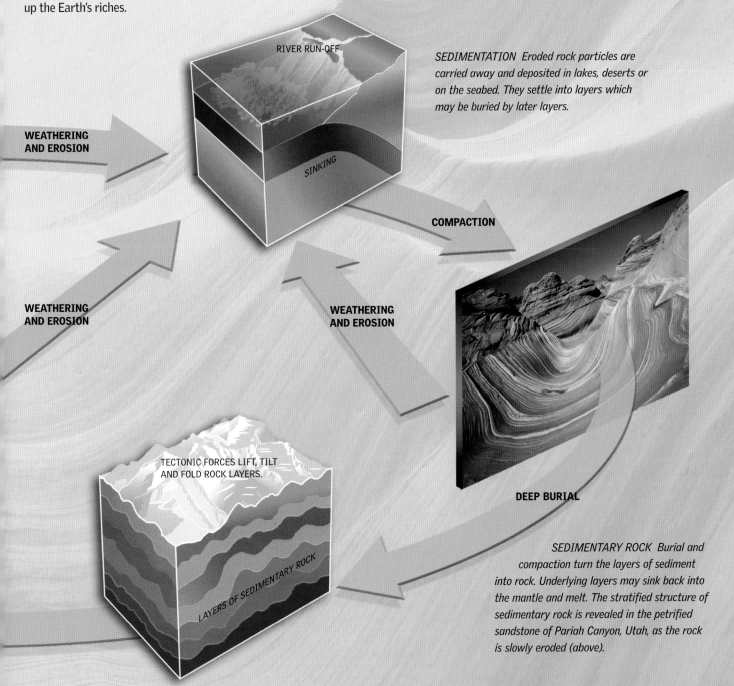

RIVER RUN-OFF

WEATHERING AND EROSION

SINKING

SEDIMENTATION Eroded rock particles are carried away and deposited in lakes, deserts or on the seabed. They settle into layers which may be buried by later layers.

WEATHERING AND EROSION

WEATHERING AND EROSION

COMPACTION

TECTONIC FORCES LIFT, TILT AND FOLD ROCK LAYERS.

LAYERS OF SEDIMENTARY ROCK

DEEP BURIAL

SEDIMENTARY ROCK Burial and compaction turn the layers of sediment into rock. Underlying layers may sink back into the mantle and melt. The stratified structure of sedimentary rock is revealed in the petrified sandstone of Pariah Canyon, Utah, as the rock is slowly eroded (above).

MAGNETIC EARTH

DEEP IN THE HEART OF THE PLANET, THE METAL-RICH CORE IS RESPONSIBLE FOR PRODUCING THE EARTH'S MAGNETIC FIELD. The solid inner core, which at 5000°C is almost as hot as the surface of the Sun, is constantly rotating, and as it does so the liquid iron in the outer core churns and seethes against it. The rotation of the core is only slightly faster than that of the Earth, but the movement of the liquid iron acts like the spinning conductor of a dynamo, creating an electrical current that produces a magnetic field around the planet. From the pattern of the field lines, it looks as though there is a huge bar magnet inside the Earth. The magnetic poles do not quite align with the rotational axis of the Earth, which results in the magnetic north pole inclining from the geographic north pole by 11 degrees.

Patterns from the past

With Earth's liquid outer core churning against the inner core, the magnetic field tends to be somewhat variable and the magnetic poles appear to 'wander', moving about on a daily basis and travelling several kilometres in the course of a year. If it continues in its current direction and speed, the north magnetic pole, which is currently in Canada, could be in Siberia by 2050, although it would be wrong to assume that this will happen.

Every so often, movement in the liquid outer core reaches a tipping point, the direction of the magnetic field flips over and the poles swap places. Scientists discovered the phenomenon when they examined iron-rich rocks at the edges of spreading plates, such as the mid-Atlantic ridge. As two plates move apart,

magma is deposited on either side of the boundary. The iron atoms in the magma are magnetic and align with Earth's magnetic field as the rock cools. Once the rock solidifies, the alignment is fixed. By examining successive bands of rock on the ocean bed, geologists discovered that the magnetic poles change polarity every so often. The rate at which they reverse appears to be random, and the last change occurred 780 000 years ago. We do not know when we are due for another flip, or what that would mean, except that compasses would point south.

Lights in the sky

Earth's magnetic field extends out into space in the magnetosphere. This deflects most of the solar wind, a stream of charged particles emanating from the Sun, but some particles are channelled into the Earth's atmosphere at the magnetic poles. Here they interact with atmospheric gases to produce a display of coloured lights, called aurorae. In the Northern Hemisphere the display is known as the aurora borealis, or northern lights; in the Southern Hemisphere, as the aurora australis.

The lights take many forms – enormous billowing sheets, pillars, wisps and haloes of luminous green or pink, yellow or crimson. The Inuit believed the lights were their ancestors playing with a walrus skull, while Norse legend says that the phenomenon arises from light reflected from the shields of the Valkyries, Odin's handmaidens, as they rode across the sky.

A large solar flare, or outburst of radiation from the Sun, can sometimes cause a geomagnetic storm within the magnetosphere. Such storms can interfere with radio waves and satellite communications, and may even affect power lines. Astronomers now monitor this 'space weather' and can give a day or two's warning of an impending storm. Those who might be affected can halt their activities, while aurorae fans can get into position for a fabulous show.

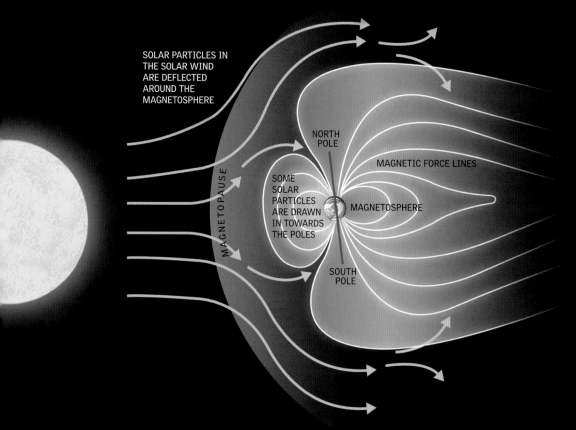

SOLAR PARTICLES IN THE SOLAR WIND ARE DEFLECTED AROUND THE MAGNETOSPHERE

MAGNETOPAUSE

NORTH POLE

MAGNETIC FORCE LINES

SOME SOLAR PARTICLES ARE DRAWN IN TOWARDS THE POLES

MAGNETOSPHERE

SOUTH POLE

PROTECTIVE FIELD The magnetosphere protects the Earth from the solar wind, which would otherwise strip away the atmosphere and most surface water. On the side facing the Sun, the magnetosphere is flattened where it meets the solar wind. The boundary, or magnetopause, is 69 000 km from Earth. On the other side, the tail stretches away for 12.5 million km. Most charged particles are deflected, but some travel along magnetic force lines towards the poles.

AURORA BOREALIS Solar particles collide with gas molecules high in the atmosphere above Canada, producing a swirling curtain of coloured lights in the sky.

GEOTHERMAL ENERGY

FOR AT LEAST 10 000 YEARS, PEOPLE HAVE MADE USE OF THE NATURALLY OCCURRING AND ABUNDANT HEAT GENERATED WITHIN THE EARTH. The ancient Native Americans used geothermally heated water for cooking, as did the Maoris of New Zealand, and the Romans used it for heating their buildings. People have always used hot springs for bathing and relaxing, and taken the mineral-rich waters in the hope of improving their health. During the 20th century, technology was developed for harnessing geothermal energy on a large scale, as a direct source of heat, for electricity generation and for a number of agricultural and industrial processes. As the underground water supply is constantly being replaced by rain or snow, and the heat is being created continuously within the Earth, geothermal energy is renewable, although some sources become inactive at times.

Geothermal reservoirs of water and steam occur all over the world in places where hot magma rises close to the Earth's surface. This can happen along plate boundaries, in areas where there are cracks and fissures in the rock and in places where the crust has thinned. As heat travels outwards through rocks in the crust, water stored in the more porous rocks is heated, producing energy in the form of steam and hot water. In places, large reservoirs of heat or steam are trapped beneath the surface rock. To be accessible, a reservoir needs to be at a depth of 3 km or less below ground. Wells are drilled through the rock to harness the energy.

In some places, geothermal energy breaks through the surface naturally. The impressive eruptions of geysers occur where hot water from deep below ground rises up through a series of constrictions in the rock. As water collects in a chamber, constriction builds up the pressure, forcing the water through to the next chamber. When the hot water eventually erupts at the surface, a corresponding drop in pressure in the hotter water at greater depths prompts a series of violent steam explosions. These expand the volume of the now boiling water by more than 1500 times, and a tall plume of superheated water finally bursts into the open. The frequency of such eruptions depends on the time that the underground chambers take to fill.

Although there is an abundance of geothermal energy inside the Earth, it is only accessible in certain places. The largest reserves occur in regions where there is a high level of volcanic activity, such as the western USA, Iceland, New Zealand and Japan. Only in such places are the supplies large enough and close enough to the surface to be worth exploiting for geothermal power plants.

As heat travels outwards through rocks in the crust, water stored in porous rock is heated, producing energy in the form of steam and hot water. In places, large reservoirs of heat or steam are trapped beneath the surface rock.

HOT BATH Iceland's Blue Lagoon is formed from excess water pumped up for the Svartsengi geothermal power plant. The temperature in the areas where people bathe averages 40°C.

Steam-driven turbines

Geothermal resources are classified by temperature: less than 90°C is low, 90–150°C is moderate, above 150°C is high. Low and moderate sources can be used in direct-heat systems and heat pumps, while high-temperature sources are used to generate electricity. Direct-heat systems take hot water from a geothermal reservoir via a borehole. The water delivers heat directly or indirectly via a heat exchanger. The cooled water is then injected back into the ground so that the water supply is not depleted.

In geothermal power plants, the Earth's heat is used to power the turbines that generate electricity. There are three different systems. Most plants use the steam-flash system, which utilises water reservoirs. Extremely hot water – at temperatures of over 180°C – flows up through wells under its own pressure, turning into steam as it reaches the surface. The steam is used to power turbines. Another method is the dry-steam system, which involves drawing very hot steam, above 235°C, from a steam reservoir and piping it directly to the turbines that generate electricity. Used steam, in the form of condensed water, goes into the plant's cooling system and is returned into the ground. The third system is the binary-cycle power plant, which uses cooler water than the flash system, 110–180°C, to heat a fluid with a lower boiling point than water. The fluid vaporises, and the vapour provides the energy to power turbines.

FACTS

'THE GEYSERS' IN NORTHERN CALIFORNIA IS THE LARGEST complex of geothermal power plants in the world. Twenty-one power plants positioned over steam reservoirs in an area covering 78 km² generate 750 megawatts of electricity – enough to power a city the size of San Francisco.

87 PER CENT of homes in Iceland are heated using a geothermal direct-heat system.

GEOTHERMAL RESERVOIRS can reach a temperature of 537°C.

FACTS

OLD FAITHFUL

ONE OF THE MOST THRILLING DISPLAYS

OF THE EARTH'S GEOTHERMAL POWER is at Old Faithful geyser in Yellowstone National Park. The name is misleading – it's not that reliable and you couldn't set your watch by it. Nevertheless, visitors need not wait long for the geyser to produce a spectacular explosion of scalding water and steam. The fountain shoots 30 m into the air, towering over the mineral-encrusted surroundings.

Yellowstone is a thermal wonderland of geysers, mudpots and hot springs. It lies over an ancient volcano that last erupted 640 000 years ago, and the hot springs and geysers respond to the seismic processes going on below. Old Faithful was christened in 1870 by members of the Washburn expedition, who noticed its regular eruptions. Its average interval is 74 minutes, but eruptions occur any time between 45 and 110 minutes apart. Some people believe that Old Faithful can predict an earthquake in the area, its interval extending before the impending shudder.

HEIGHT: 30-55 m
WATER TEMPERATURE: 95.6°C
STEAM TEMPERATURE: 180°C
VOLUME OF WATER EXPELLED:
   14 000–32 000 litres
DURATION OF ERUPTION: 1.5 to
   5 minutes
INTERVAL BETWEEN ERUPTIONS:
   45–110 minutes

The first commercial geothermal power plant was built in 1913 in Larderello, Italy. Today, there are geothermal power plants in more than 20 countries, including North America, New Zealand and Iceland. They are also proving successful in Kenya's Rift Valley. The current global geothermal generation capacity is about 8000 megawatts in total.

Land of fire and ice

Nowhere in the world does geothermal energy play a greater role than in Iceland. Geothermal energy was first exploited there at the turn of the 20th century when farmers began using naturally produced hot steam to heat their homes. By 1930, a district heating system was built to use the 87°C water from hot springs at Laugardalir, Reykjavik, to heat a local school. Today, 87 per cent of homes in Iceland are heated by geothermal direct heating, while in 2006 Iceland produced more than 25 per cent of its electricity from geothermal sources.

Though Iceland's terrain may be covered in snow and ice, just below the surface there is intense heat, manifested in the region's numerous hot springs, geysers and more than 100 active volcanoes. Iceland owes this geothermal abundance to its location on the Mid-Atlantic Ridge. A mid-ocean ridge forms when two oceanic plates, in this case the Eurasian and North American plates, are moving slowly apart. Cracks in the Earth's crust allow magma to rise to the surface and spew out. Most mid-ocean ridges occur deep beneath the sea, but Iceland happens to be above a hotspot – a place where a plume of hot magma is rising up and heating the outer layer of the Earth. The plume of magma pushes the crust upwards, lifting Iceland above sea level. One of the most important uses of geothermal energy in Iceland, apart

from residential heating, is for heating greenhouses. In 2002, the area of greenhouses amounted to nearly 200 000 m², roughly half growing vegetables and half growing flowers. Geothermal energy is also used for drying vegetables and fish, while the diatomite plant at Lake Myvatn uses more than 200 000 tonnes of steam a year to extract and process 27 000 tonnes of diatomite, a sedimentary deposit of microscopic plants that has a number of industrial uses in the food-processing, pharmaceutical and chemical industries.

Ground heat

Although the harnessing of geothermal energy for large-scale power generation is only viable in certain places, on a small scale it can provide energy almost anywhere in the world. All over the globe, the ground in the top 3 m of the Earth's surface stays at a relatively constant temperature of 10–16°C. Heat pumps can capture this energy and use it to heat or cool buildings indirectly.

Fluid – usually water or a mixture of water and antifreeze – is pumped through a long, looping system of pipes buried underground. In winter, the ground is warmer than the buildings above; the fluid absorbs heat, and as it circulates through a heat exchanger, this heat is removed and pumped into the building. In summer the system works in reverse: heat from indoors passes through the heat exchanger and is used to heat water for the building's hot-water system, or is cooled underground.

NATURAL HEAT The Svartsengi power plant in Iceland produces clean electricity and hot water for heating.

NUCLEAR ENERGY

IN 1789, THE GERMAN CHEMIST MARTIN KLAPROTH SEPARATED A YELLOWISH OXIDE FROM A BROWNISH-BLACK MINERAL CALLED PITCHBLENDE. He named the new substance uranium after the planet Uranus, which had been discovered eight years earlier. He had no idea that it held the key to a new and potent source of energy, or that it would one day be harnessed as a weapon of unprecedented destruction.

Uranium is the heaviest naturally occurring element on Earth. It is widely distributed throughout the mantle and crust, being 40 times more abundant than silver, and is even found in seawater. Its usual concentration of around 2–4 parts per million (ppm) is so low that it is not worth recovering, but in some parts of the world the movement and reburial of rocks over millions of years has created uranium-rich mineral deposits. Secondary ore bodies, which are generally less concentrated, have formed where the primary ore was washed out and deposited in sediments. Uranium ores that are currently exploited are usually concentrated to more than 350 ppm.

The world's largest producer of uranium is Canada, which produces roughly a third of the world's uranium supplies, closely followed by Australia. According to the

TWO VIEWS OF URANIUM Pitchblende (above) is one of many minerals in which uranium is found in its natural state. Open-cast uranium mines (below) dot the Koongarra region of Australia's Kakadu National Park, which is rich in uranium reserves.

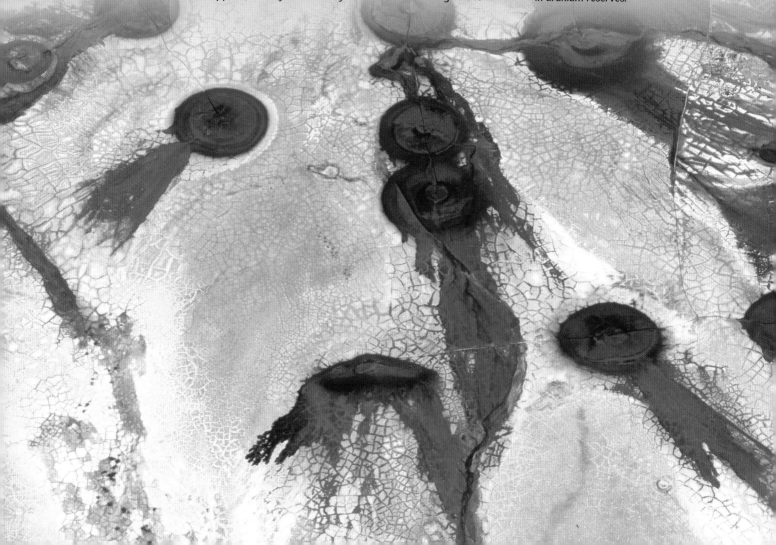

World Nuclear Association, Canada produced nearly 14 000 tonnes of uranium oxide in 2005, and Australia 11 000 tonnes. Of the two countries, Australia has the greater reserves, estimated at 1.143 million tonnes – almost three times that of Canada. Other countries with significant uranium reserves include Kazakhstan, the USA, South Africa, Namibia, Brazil and Russia.

A radioactive metal

In 1896, French physicist Henri Becquerel accidentally left a sample of uranium salts on top of an unexposed photographic plate. When he developed the plate, he saw a faint image of the sample and concluded that invisible rays of energy must be emanating from the uranium. He called them 'Becquerel rays'. Today, we call them nuclear radiation because, as Bequerel went on to deduce, the radiation arises from the nucleus of the uranium atoms.

Uranium nuclei are unstable; they disintegrate at random, giving out tiny particles of matter (alpha particles). The process is called radioactive decay, and it releases heat. Although the radioactivity is very small, the large quantity of uranium spread throughout the Earth is enough to contribute at least half of the planet's internal heat.

Like other elements, uranium exists in slightly different forms, called isotopes. There are three naturally occurring uranium isotopes: uranium-238 (U-238), U-235 and U-234. U-235 is the only naturally occurring isotope that can be readily split, or fissioned, giving out large amounts of energy in the process. In theory, 1 kg of uranium can produce about 20 trillion joules of energy when it is fully fissioned. The fissile nature of U-235 is the reason that uranium is such a highly valued resource today, for weapons and for fuelling power plants.

Mining uranium

Before being used in a nuclear reactor, uranium is separated into its different isotopes so that the concentration of the most useful isotope, U-235, can be increased. This process is called 'enrichment'. The enriched uranium dioxide (normally to a concentration of 2–3 per cent) is formed into pellets that are encased in long stainless steel tubes to form fuel rods for use in nuclear reactors. Weapons grade uranium is enriched to more than 90 per cent.

Nuclear energy is often considered 'clean' because it does not release carbon dioxide into the atmosphere.

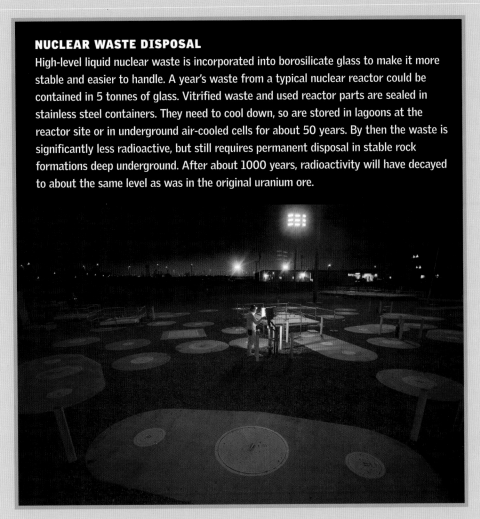

NUCLEAR WASTE DISPOSAL
High-level liquid nuclear waste is incorporated into borosilicate glass to make it more stable and easier to handle. A year's waste from a typical nuclear reactor could be contained in 5 tonnes of glass. Vitrified waste and used reactor parts are sealed in stainless steel containers. They need to cool down, so are stored in lagoons at the reactor site or in underground air-cooled cells for about 50 years. By then the waste is significantly less radioactive, but still requires permanent disposal in stable rock formations deep underground. After about 1000 years, radioactivity will have decayed to about the same level as was in the original uranium ore.

According to the Uranium Information Centre, every 22 tonnes of uranium used for generating electricity save about a million tonnes of carbon dioxide that would be released if coal was burned to produce the same amount of energy. Yet nuclear energy does have a significant problem associated with its use – what to do with the radioactive waste materials that result.

In nuclear power stations, anything that has come into contact with radioactive material has to be very carefully disposed of, from the spent fuel rods to the water that circulates through the plant. In Europe, much of the spent fuel is reprocessed, by dissolving and separating it into uranium and plutonium, which is also fissile. These materials can be used again. The recycling still leaves significant amounts of concentrated and highly toxic radioactive material that must be immobilised, sealed in corrosion-resistant containers, allowed to cool down and then stored in repositories deep underground in remote locations.

Accidents such as the one at Three Mile Island in 1979 and Chernobyl in 1986 have raised public concern over the safety of nuclear power stations themselves. Though rare, such accidents can produce widespread contamination of land. Radioactive dust is carried in the atmosphere to land over a wide geographical area. After Chernobyl, for example, sheep in the North of England and reindeer in Lapland were contaminated by radioactive material that had travelled vast distances in the atmosphere.

POWER OF THE ATOM

ON AUGUST 6, 1945, THE TERRIFYING POWER THAT COULD BE RELEASED FROM THE ATOMS WITHIN JUST A SMALL AMOUNT OF MATTER WAS REVEALED TO THE WORLD when a US aircraft dropped the first atomic bomb on the Japanese city of Hiroshima. In seconds, 100 000 people were killed outright and an 18 km high mushroom cloud towered above the landscape. The city was obliterated by a massive shockwave and ferocious firestorms. Decades later the resulting radiation would still be killing people. Another bomb followed on Nagasaki, bringing the Second World War to an end. Yet the Cold War – when nations lived in fear of each other as they raced to build up huge arsenals of these deadly weapons – had just begun. The potential for weapons based on splitting the atom – or more precisely, splitting the nucleus of an atom – in a process known as nuclear fission, had been known about for some time. In 1932, Ernest Rutherford was the first scientist to split the atom, and Otto Hahn and Fritz Strassmann produced a fission chain reaction in 1938.

When free neutrons hit uranium nuclei, they split them and send out further neutrons, which hit other nuclei, creating a self-sustaining chain reaction. In sufficient quantity and left uncontrolled, this reaction can quickly lead to the explosive power of the atom bomb.

Neutrons fired at the nucleus of a uranium atom split it into fragments. As well as emitting heat energy, two more neutrons shoot out from the fragmented nucleus. These free neutrons hit other uranium nuclei, splitting them and sending out further neutrons, creating a self-sustaining chain reaction. In sufficient quantity and left uncontrolled, this reaction can quickly lead to the explosive power of the atom bomb. When the reaction takes place at a controlled rate inside a nuclear reactor, the energy can be harnessed to generate power. Today, most of the uranium mined around the world ends up as fuel for nuclear reactors.

Electricity generation

The first commercial nuclear power stations began operating in the 1950s. Like coal or gas-fired power stations, they use heat to turn water into steam, and the steam drives the turbines that generate electricity. There are various designs of nuclear reactors, but the most widely used type for generating electricity is called a pressurised water reactor. In the heart of the reactor the fuel rods (containing enriched uranium) are

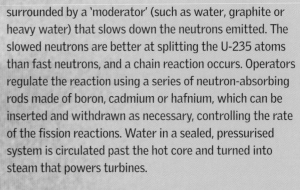

surrounded by a 'moderator' (such as water, graphite or heavy water) that slows down the neutrons emitted. The slowed neutrons are better at splitting the U-235 atoms than fast neutrons, and a chain reaction occurs. Operators regulate the reaction using a series of neutron-absorbing rods made of boron, cadmium or hafnium, which can be inserted and withdrawn as necessary, controlling the rate of the fission reactions. Water in a sealed, pressurised system is circulated past the hot core and turned into steam that powers turbines.

Little Boy's big brothers

The atomic bomb dropped on Hiroshima, code-named Little Boy, was powered by the fission of uranium. The bombs developed subsequently use a far more deadly technology – that of fusion. Known as hydrogen bombs, they are a thousand times more powerful. The first one was tested by the USA in 1952.

Hydrogen bombs rely on the fusion of two isotopes of hydrogen to form helium atoms – the same process as happens within the Sun and other stars (see page 34). Extreme temperatures are needed to sustain the reaction – between 50 million°C and 400 million°C, depending on the isotopes used – and this is produced by using an atomic fission bomb as the trigger. The chain reaction that is set in motion continues until the energy released becomes so great that the bomb blows itself apart. The explosion of a hydrogen bomb creates a hot zone at the centre of the blast where nearly all matter is vaporised into a high-pressure gas. This gas forces its way outwards in the form of a shockwave, causing most of the destruction wrought by the bomb.

A second type of fusion-fission bomb, called a neutron bomb, was developed in the 1970s. The bomb is detonated above ground and its energy is released as a blast of high-energy neutrons designed to kill organic life with radiation, rather than to destroy buildings through shockwaves or heat.

WEAPONS TEST This test of a nuclear artillery shell took place in the Nevada desert in 1953. The energy released sent a cloud of hot gases and debris mushrooming into the sky.

FUSION FUTURE

SINCE THE DEVELOPMENT OF HYDROGEN BOMBS IN THE 1950S, SCIENTISTS HAVE SOUGHT A MORE ALTRUISTIC USE FOR THE IMMENSE POWER OF NUCLEAR FUSION. If such power could be harnessed, it would provide an almost limitless source of energy. Yet there is a big difference between letting off a bomb and controlling a reaction that normally occurs at the centre of the Sun. Scientists at the Joint European Torus (JET) at the Culham Science Centre, near Oxford, have been working on the problem since 1983, and they think they are almost there.

The fuel used in a fusion reactor consists of two types of hydrogen isotope – deuterium and tritium. When they are forced together they form helium. The reaction gives out much more energy than the fission reactions used in conventional nuclear reactors. For the fusion energy to be harnessed, more efficient reactions are required than occur in the Sun, and temperatures in excess of 100 million °C are needed to achieve them. In comparison, the core of the Sun is 15 million °C. The heat turns the deuterium and tritium into a super-hot plasma gas in which the particles are so hot that they overcome their natural repulsion and collide in the elusive fusion reaction. So the key to utilising fusion lies in working out how to maintain and control the high-temperature plasmas.

Limitless energy

JET uses a Tokamak, the most advanced fusion reactor. It is doughnut-shaped, with a 2800 tonne iron core and numerous enormous magnets spaced around the chamber. Scientists use the strong magnetic fields produced to isolate the plasma and ensure that it does not touch the chamber walls, where it would lose heat. The plasma particles spiral around inside the doughnut, following the field lines of the magnets, and hopefully collide. The machine is something of a power drain – just one JET pulse uses about 700 megawatts of electricity. The aim is to produce more energy from fusion than is used by the machine itself. Currently, JET produces 70 per cent of the power needed to heat the plasma.

JET has produced fusion reactions that have been maintained for around five seconds. In 1997 it produced a peak of 16.1 megawatts of fusion power, with power of over 10 megawatts sustained for over 0.5 sec. This is a long way below the output required from a power station, although work at JET has paved the way for a larger and more powerful machine. The International Thermonuclear Experimental Reactor, which is to be built at Cadarache in France, will be ten times bigger than JET.

Though the holy grail of a fusion power station remains decades away, the energy potential is enormous. Just 10 g of deuterium (easily obtained from 500 litres of water) and 15 g of tritium (produced from 30 g of lithium) would produce enough energy to last the average Westerner a lifetime.

HEAT MACHINE The JET experimental fusion reactor heats plasma to higher temperatures than occur in the Sun.

STORED ENERGY

3

WE NEED ENERGY TO SURVIVE, AND IN THE MODERN AGE THE QUEST FOR IT IS AN EVER MORE PRESSING CONCERN. Fortunately, the Earth abounds in stored energy, from the wood that grows around us to the reserves of oil and natural gas hidden beneath some of the harshest environments on our planet, such as the tundra of this remote corner of Siberia (left). We can tap the energy stored in crops by turning them into biofuels. Or we can dig for it, literally, as coal miners do. At the root of all this energy is sunlight. Even fossil fuels – coal, oil and gas – were formed from organic material. Prehistoric microorganisms and plants captured sunlight and over time their remains, subjected to heat and pressure, were transformed into the concentrated sources of energy we know and use today. We don't lack for energy, but we do need to shepherd our resources wisely.

WOOD

MORE THAN A MILLION YEARS AGO, OUR DISTANT FOREBEARS LEARNED HOW TO MAKE FIRE, and ever since wood has been fundamental to human life. For thousands of years, it was our dominant source of energy, and while populations were relatively small, an abundant one. People burned it for heating and cooking; without it there would have been no charcoal to use in industries such as smelting iron and firing pottery. It has been crucial to the continuing technological development that has marked human history.

It is still a vital fuel. According to the UN's Food and Agriculture Organization, more than 2 billion people worldwide depend on wood for cooking, heating and food preservation. In fact, in many countries demand for fuel wood and charcoal is rising, especially in urban areas. The largest consumers are the Asian nations (48 per cent), followed by Africa (31 per cent). Western countries became less dependent on wood as a fuel in the 19th century, when coal became the dominant source of energy, later superseded by oil and gas. In most industrialised countries today, wood accounts for a small percentage – 3 or 4 per cent – of the energy consumed. But even in the West, it is making a comeback in some places as a fuel. Sweden, for example, has abundant reserves of wood in well-managed forests. As part of a bid to reduce its dependency on oil, it has opened a number of small power plants that burn wood to generate electricity.

WILLOW STACKS Willow has been grown and cropped for centuries in regions such as the Somerset Levels (above) in western England. The 'withies' (long, flexible twigs) are used for basketwork and today also for fuel.

Carbon neutral

As a fuel, wood has many advantages, particularly in an age when we need to reduce carbon dioxide emissions. It is 'carbon neutral' – the amount of carbon dioxide released when wood from a tree is burned is equal to the amount of carbon taken out of the atmosphere when the tree grew. Carbon emissions from burning wood are in any case much lower than those for fossil fuels, especially when using modern combustion stoves. For every unit of energy produced when wood is burned, the wood gives out about ten times less carbon dioxide than coal, gas or oil does.

It does, however, have to be used sustainably. This means managing woodlands so that trees harvested for fuel are replaced by planting new trees. When this happens, wood is a renewable resource, while the managed woodlands also benefit wildlife. And they don't have to be vast forests. One convenient method of producing wood for fuel is to grow coppices of densely planted, high-yielding varieties of poplar or willow, called short rotation coppices, which are harvested every three to five years. The stems are cut and chipped (turned into wood chips) in a single operation; the wood chips can then be stored or burned for heat or electricity production. The coppice stools (stumps) remain productive for 30 years before they need to be replaced.

Unfortunately, in many of the regions that depend most on wood for fuel, woodlands are disappearing at an alarming rate. This is partly a result of expanding populations burning more and more wood without replanting trees, although other factors are involved, such as forests being cleared and the land used to raise crops. Whatever the cause, woodlands are being lost – and with serious consequences.

One place to have suffered in this way is the Sahel, the African region skirting the southern Sahara. Here, woodlands have vanished so rapidly that people in some towns have to travel 100 km or more to find firewood. The loss of woodland has also contributed to desertification of the region. But it is possible to reverse the trend, as

has happened in parts of the Sahel where Western aid agencies have encouraged local people to protect tree saplings rather than cut them down. Traditionally, farmers removed saplings sprouting in their fields before sowing their crops. Now, many plough around them and nurture them. A key factor has been a change in legislation in countries such as Mali and Niger, where trees were once regarded as state property. Now, they belong to the farmers on whose land they grow, so the farmers have an incentive to look after them. As a result of one such scheme, tree cover has sprung back in some 3 million hectares of south-eastern Niger. The trees help to prevent erosion and hold water in the soil, and the farmers profit in many ways, including selling branches for firewood. Fuel wood is no longer in such short supply, and the wider environmental benefits are immense.

THE WOOD-CARRIERS In African villages, gathering firewood is a vital and often daily task, frequently done (as here in Niger) by women. When wood is scarce, the women have to go farther to find it, which takes more time out of their day, leaving them less time for other important tasks.

BIO FUEL

THE FERTILE PLAINS OF THE US MIDWEST ARE OFTEN CALLED THE NATION'S BREAD BASKET, but these days the term 'fuel bucket' is becoming more appropriate. Farmers there are growing vast acres of corn (maize) with the sole purpose of turning it into a colourless alcohol called ethanol, a biofuel that can be used to run cars and other vehicles.

A biofuel revolution is taking place. In the USA, petrol containing 10 per cent ethanol, called E-10, is now used in many urban areas. There are also an increasing number of flex-fuel vehicles (FFVs) with special engines that can use up to 85 per cent ethanol (E-85). Today, out of a total 200 million cars on the US roads, 6 million are FFVs.

Turning crops into fuels

Any crop high in carbohydrates can be turned into ethanol, including barley, wheat, rice, sunflower, sugar cane and sugar beet. The plants are pulped and the mash is fermented with yeasts and the starchy component turned into sugars and then ethanol. Scientists are also researching ways of making ethanol from cellulose, a fibre that makes up the bulk of most plant material. Once they have found an economical way of doing this, it will be possible to make ethanol from trees, grasses and any kind of crop waste.

The most appropriate crop for a given country depends on what grows best in its climate. In the USA, it is corn. According to the Renewable Fuels Association, the USA now has

DIESEL CROP Oilseed rape covers the rolling landscape of South Africa's Western Cape province. Oil extracted from the seeds can be used to make biodiesel.

PATTY CAKES There is nothing new about biofuels, which can take many forms. In India, people have for centuries used cakes of dried cow dung as a fuel for cooking.

110 biorefineries able to make more than 22 000 million litres of ethanol a year. Most production is in Iowa, Nebraska and Illinois.

In Brazil, where the ethanol industry is particularly advanced, the best crop is sugar cane, which grows abundantly in the tropical regions. During the international oil crisis in 1975, the Brazilian government decided to reduce the country's consumption of oil by replacing all fuels derived from oil with ethanol. The Programa Nacional do Alcool (National Alcohol Programme) has been so successful that today most cars in Brazil run on pure ethanol or a mixture of 75 per cent petrol and 25 per cent ethanol.

Of all the biofuel crops, sugar cane is the most efficient for producing ethanol. After the sucrose has been removed for fermenting into ethanol, the residue, called bagasse, is burned at the biorefinery to provide heat and electricity to run the plant. This means that ethanol plants can be self-sufficient in energy and can even sell off the surplus.

Biodiesel, biomass and biogas

Another biofuel is biodiesel, made by combining vegetable oil, animal fat or even used cooking oil with methanol, a type of alcohol. Europe is currently the largest producer and user, followed by the USA. In Europe, the oil used is extracted from oilseed rape; in the USA, soybean oil and recycled restauraunt grease are used. Biodiesel is usually blended with diesel at a concentration of 2 per cent, 5 per cent or 20 per cent.

In fact, all organic waste – or biomass – contains energy, and that includes municipal waste, such as leftover food, hedge clippings and leaves. In waste-to-energy power plants, the energy is released by burning the rubbish to turn water into steam, used as a source of heating or to generate electricity. The countries that capture the most energy from their rubbish are Denmark (which burns 54 per cent of its rubbish in waste-to-energy plants), Switzerland (which burns 50 per cent) and France (which burns 43 per cent).

There are some disadvantages, however. Biomass gives out less energy than coal – roughly a quarter, weight for weight. It also releases harmful substances in the waste. Strict regulations have to be imposed to prevent potentially dangerous gases and particulates from being released into the atmosphere and to ensure that the ash residue is disposed of safely. But in spite of these drawbacks, burning waste has one key advantage: it means that less rubbish has to be buried in landfill sites. This is important since we are simply running out of space for new sites.

Another way of getting energy from rubbish is by capturing the methane gas released as biomass decomposes. In some landfills, the methane is collected for use as a fuel. This has the benefit of reducing the amount of methane released into the atmosphere, which would otherwise add to greenhouse gases.

COAL PORTERS *Chinese labourers load baskets of coal onto a barge in the Chang Jiang (Yangtze River). China is by far the world's largest user of coal, consuming a colossal 1191.3 million tonnes in 2006.*

COAL AND PEAT

COAL LOOKS LIKE HARD, BLACK LUMPS OF ROCK, but actually it is made from the remains of plants that lived and died millions of years ago. Confirming its origins, immaculate plant fossils are sometimes found within coal seams. Miners have chanced upon beautiful specimens of prehistoric ferns and even whole trees. They have also come across traces of the creatures that once roamed ancient marshy forest floors.

The oldest, hardest coal was formed in the Carboniferous period, 360–280 million years ago, but later seams were laid down 250–200 million years ago in the Triassic period. This was the age of the dinosaurs, and occasionally one of these seams carries dinosaur footprints or even fossils. In 1878, miners unearthed 38 iguanodon fossils at Bernissart in Belgium, among the first complete specimens ever recovered. Being intact, the skeletons allowed palaeontologists to determine how the bones fitted together and what the iguanodons would have looked like when they were alive.

Coal starts as plants growing in swampy deltas and peat bogs. Deposits of silt and sediments bury the plant remains and, over millions of years, subject them to high temperatures and pressure. This results in physical and chemical changes that eventually create coal, the quality of a deposit depending on the temperature, pressure and length of time it took to form.

The youngest coal is lignite or brown coal, which is relatively soft, with a high moisture content (30–40 per cent) and the lowest energy content. It is typically used for electricity generation. After millions more years, lignite turns into sub-bituminous coal. In time, this becomes harder and blacker, forming bituminous or hard coal, with a moisture content of less than 20 per cent. This is used by industry and to make coke. The hardest coal of all, anthracite, is the product of further high temperatures and pressure. It is black and shiny, and its moisture content is less than 15 per cent. With the highest carbon content, it is the most energy-rich coal.

*BROWN AND BLACK
Grades of coal range
from soft lignite – used
in electricity generating
stations – to the highest-
quality anthracite, the
hardest coal, burned in
domestic fireplaces.*

LIGNITE OR BROWN COAL

ANTHRACITE

Rich reserves

Coal is widely distributed across the globe, and it was the first fossil fuel humans exploited as a source of energy. It is found in more than 70 countries, with the largest reserves in the United States, Russia, China and India. In 2006, BP estimated that more than 900 million tonnes of 'proven' reserves (known to be in the ground and exploitable) existed worldwide. At current rates of production, these would last 150 years. But this figure does not include undetected reserves or deposits that have not been fully mapped, so there is probably much more recoverable coal in the world.

Initially, people collected coal from beaches, where it had been washed from cliffs or the seabed, or they took it from places where it was naturally exposed on the surface. The Chinese first mined for coal about 3000 years ago in the north-east of their country, and they remained the world's biggest producers of coal until the 18th century. In the West, coal fuelled the Industrial Revolution, powering the first steam engines, as well as generating the heat needed to smelt iron and make steel and other alloys. In 1882, the American inventor, Thomas Edison, built the first coal-fired station for generating electricity to power the household lights of New York. By 2002, coal provided 39 per cent of the world's electricity.

The first mines were bell pits, formed by digging a relatively shallow shaft to reach the coal layer. The coal was extracted in a bell-shaped chamber around the bottom of the hole. Eventually, the shaft would become unstable, then the pit would be abandoned and another one sunk nearby. But as reserves that could be reached in this way were used up, the shafts had to go deeper and deeper. Conditions in the deep-shaft mines were hazardous, with the danger of flooding from groundwater, shaft collapse, explosions and poisonous gases. In the earliest days the mines often relied on the labour of children, who were sent down from the age of six as 'trappers' or

*DINOSAUR FOOTPRINTS Herbivorous dinosaurs called
ankylosaurs left these and other tracks at the Smoky
River coal mine in the foothills of the Canadian Rockies.*

'trammers'. Trappers opened and shut traps (canvas flaps or doors) that directed the mine's ventilation as wagons of coal passed through them; trammers dragged carts of coal through low tunnels.

In Britain, the Mines Act of 1842 made it illegal to employ children under the age of ten (later raised to 12) down the mines. At this time, Britain was a world leader in coal production. In 1913, when the the British coal industry reached its peak, there were more than a million miners working in the country in more than 3000 mines, producing 290 million tonnes a year.

For extracting the coal, the pillar and stall method was often used. Miners tunnelled into the coal seams, leaving a series of coal pillars to support the mine's roof. When they had extracted the bulk of the coal from the seam, they took the coal from the pillars and allowed the roof to collapse as they retreated. Another more expensive method, generally used nowadays, is longwall mining. In this system, coal is excavated from a coal face, which can be more than 300 m long. The miners

dig a deep slot beneath the seam, which then collapses into the slot under its own weight or with the help of explosives. Before mechanisation took off in the 1930s, longwall mining was an extremely dangerous occupation, as miners had to use hand picks to dig (or 'hole') out the slot. Sudden falls of coal were frequent during 'holing out', often killing or injuring miners.

When coal is near the surface, open-cast mining is possible. This is much safer than underground mining and recovers a greater percentage of coal (typically 90 per cent). Essentially, the miners are quarrying the coal, as in a stone or gravel quarry. The overlying rock is usually broken up using explosives and excavated with large machines. Once the seam of coal has been exposed, it is removed in strips. The quality of the coal in these shallower deposits is generally poorer than that of deeper, older deposits, but productivity is high and the coal is suitable for power stations. The world's biggest open-cast mine is the Black Thunder Mine in the Powder River Basin, Wyoming, USA, which in 2006 produced 84 million tonnes of low-sulphur, sub-bituminous coal.

In the British Isles, peat bogs are some of the most important sites for wildlife, described by Prince Charles as the islands' 'tropical rainforests' because of the number and diversity of creatures they support.

PEAT FOR FUEL

IF PEAT WERE BURIED AND LEFT FOR A FEW MILLION YEARS, IT WOULD TURN INTO COAL. It is dead plant material that has accumulated in waterlogged conditions over a comparatively short period of a few thousand years. The water keeps out oxygen, which deters microorganisms such as fungi and bacteria. These would otherwise go to work on the dead plants making them decompose. It typically takes ten years for 1 cm

of peat to form, although the dynamics of peatlands vary with differences in climate, soil type and native plant species.

Peat can be classified by its colour, composition, water content or the amount of nutrients it contains. In Ireland, turf-cutters traditionally classified it by its colour, as this indicated its fuel value – the darker the peat, the greater its potential as fuel.

Conservation issues

Most peatlands are found in the northern temperate regions of the globe. They are a unique habitat, valued as an ecological resource for the great diversity of plants and animals that live in them. Indeed, in the British Isles, peat bogs are some of the most important sites for wildlife, described by Prince Charles as the islands' 'tropical rainforests' because of the number and diversity of creatures they support. At Thorne Moors near Doncaster, for

example, more than 3000 species of invertebrates have been recorded, as well as numerous birds, including the rare European nightjar, rufus nightingale, whinchat and tree pipit. Reptiles such as adders, grass snakes and common lizards are present, as well as roe deer, foxes, brown hares and water voles.

Although peat is continually being formed, the rate is very slow – about 1 mm per year – so it must be considered as a non-renewable resource. Efforts to conserve peatlands, however, are in competition with commercial demand for peat as fuel and also as a popular growing medium in horticulture. In 1971, the Ramsar Convention was agreed – at the Caspian Sea resort of Ramsar in Iran – with the aim of protecting 1651 wetland sites including peatlands across the world, covering an area of 150 million hectares. So far 154 countries have signed up, including Australia, Canada, China, Russia, the UK and the USA.

PEAT FOR FIRE Peat blocks have been stacked to dry in the air in Shetland off the north of Scotland. This is called sod peat, mostly used as household fuel.

FACTS

UNTIL 1986, MINERS OFTEN TOOK CANARIES INTO PITS.
Pockets of methane and carbon monoxide are one of the dangers of working underground, and canaries are very sensitive to low concentrations of them. If the birds showed signs of distress, it was a signal to evacuate. Now, miners carry portable electronic gas detectors.

HEALTH RESORTS in Germany offer bathing in a steaming mixture of peat and water. The peat is believed to hold cleansing properties.

FISHERMEN AND THIEVES TRADITIONALLY carried a lump of coal for good luck.

FACTS

AT THE START OF THE 21ST CENTURY, THE GLOBAL THIRST FOR OIL IS SUCH THAT WE CONSUME 83 MILLION BARRELS OF IT EVERY DAY. So many things come from this thick black liquid that it is hard to imagine life without it. We use petrol to run our cars, petroleum-based aviation fuel to fly our planes, diesel for our boats, trains and trucks, asphalt to surface our highways, and then there are the many petrochemical products, including plastics, synthetic fibres, detergents and agrochemicals – all of them made using oil.

OIL

There is a natural abundance and energy about the substance, symbolised by the 'gushers' – huge black fountains of the liquid – which sometimes shot forth from the Earth in the early days of oil prospecting and discovery.

One of the most famous and spectacular of these gushers began on March 15, 1910, when the US Union Oil company was drilling at a site outside Taft in Kern County, California. It lasted an astonishing 18 months. Workers had reached a depth of more than 600 m, but the well they were drilling had yielded only a little natural gas and no oil. Work continued, when suddenly there was a tremendous roar. In an instant, a thick column of oil shot 60 m high in the air, blowing the drill out of the bore hole. Soon, a black river was flowing over the land, and workers were scurrying around trying to contain it with sandbags.

Oil comes from the remains of microscopic plankton that fell to the seabed more than 300 million years ago. Over time, temperature and pressure turned the organic material into a waxy substance called kerogen, then to crude oil and finally gas.

OIL FLOWS Rich reserves of oil and natural gas lie beneath the sands of the Taklamakan Desert (below) in western China. 'Nodding donkey' beam pumps (opposite) extract oil from wells in Baku, Azerbaijan.

But at Taft the flow did not die down. At first, the oil rushed out at a rate of 100 000 barrels a day. A month later, it was still spurting out 90 000 barrels a day. Workers had to build a 6 m tall embankment around the well, enclosing a 24-hectare oil lake, which finally subdued the liquid as it emerged from the hole. At last, in September 1911, the flow died down when the bottom of the hole caved in. It was the greatest gusher ever seen in the USA. A bronze plaque beside the Taft-Maricopa Highway now marks the site where oil once spouted as though the Earth itself had severed an artery.

In those days, oil seemed like a bounty without limits. Nowadays, we are increasingly aware that, although the estimated reserves are still vast, oil is a finite and non-renewable resource. We have become dangerously dependent on it, and we need to cure our addiction, because one day it is going to run out.

How oil is formed

Like coal, oil is a fossil fuel. Unlike coal, it is generally not formed from dead vegetation; it is the remains of microscopic plankton that fell to the seabed when they died more than 300 million years ago. The remains mixed with mud on the sea floor and over millions of years formed thick deposits. Later, sand and silt were laid down on top of them, burying the remains deeper and deeper. As this happened, temperature and pressure increased, turning the organic material into a waxy substance called kerogen, then to crude oil and finally gas.

Oil and natural gas are often found together and always in ancient sedimentary basins, of which there are around 600 all over the world. Saudi Arabia lies on top of what was once a huge sedimentary basin, giving it the world's richest known oil supply.

Crude oil is made up of a mixture of hydrocarbons – long chains of hydrogen and carbon molecules. These relatively light molecules make their way to the surface, slipping between mineral particles of rock. When they meet an impermeable rock, they may travel horizontally along this rock until they find a region of permeable rock and continue the ascent. Quickly passing through faults and fissures, the oil eventually reaches the surface where it seeps out in natural oil springs and tarpits.

At this point, any volatile gases will evaporate and lighter parts of the oil will be eaten by bacteria, but heavier, thicker deposits may remain. Humans have long used such natural oil springs. Native Americans living in California used the tar-like substance called asphaltum to waterproof canoes and baskets and to fix feathers to the tips of their arrows. Early European settlers in California dug open pits at the oil seeps and used the material for surfacing roads and burning in oil lamps.

Black reservoirs

The tendency of oil to find its way to the surface and evaporate means that very specific conditions are needed for an underground oil field to form and survive. The oil must quickly find its way into a reservoir rock – a highly permeable type of rock – with plenty of spaces in it to hold the hydrocarbons. Good reservoir rocks include sandstones and fractured limestones. Most importantly, there also has to be an impermeable layer of rock, called a cap rock, immediately above the reservoir rock. This layer, often a clay or mudstone, traps the hydrocarbons, allowing them to accumulate. The cap rock forms a dome shape with lower escape points round its edges. The hydrocarbons create a kind of upside-down pool in the top of the dome.

Huge pressure builds up as the hydrocarbons accumulate in the pool, and that explains the force of gushers. In the early days of oil extraction, drilling equipment wasn't as sophisticated as it is nowadays. At that time, when a drill struck oil, there was no way of containing the liquid. It simply gushed up to the surface under its own pressure. But although spectacular to look at, gushers or 'wild wells' were polluting and wasteful. In 1924, the development of blowout preventers, which cap the well head if pressure rises to dangerous levels, spelled the end of them.

PIPED OIL The 1300 km Trans-Alaska Pipeline carries oil from Prudhoe Bay on the Arctic to the port of Valdez on the Gulf of Alaska.

In those early days, prospectors relied heavily on experience and intuition in their hunt for oil – reading the landscape, looking for seeps, oil-stained rocks and even sometimes discoloured vegetation. But there was a lot of luck involved, and as time went by, oil companies wanted more than luck. They had to drill deeper and deeper to find oil, and the costs of complex drilling equipment rose accordingly.

The hunt for oil

Today, petroleum geologists spend a great deal of time analysing a site before drilling so as to avoid a costly mistake. They are looking for hydrocarbon deposits deep in the ground, and although there may be telltale signs at the surface, such as oil seeps or pockmarks on the seabed with escaping bubbles of gas, for the most part they find oil and gas deposits by employing an array of sophisticated technologies.

First, they run a gravity or magnetic survey over the area. In a gravity survey, a highly sensitive machine called a gravimeter measures changes in the Earth's gravitational field, which relates to changes in the density of the underlying rocks. In a magnetic survey, a magnetometer looks for localised changes against the

PROSPECTING BY PICTURES *Geologists examine three-dimensional seismic images of Alaskan oil sands as they seek out new reserves to exploit.*

background magnetic field of the Earth. This shows up rocks with different levels of magnetism – sedimentary rock, for example, has low magnetism. The surveys reveal areas of interest, which the geologists then investigate in more detail using seismic surveys. These determine the type of rock present by the time it takes soundwaves to travel through the rock and be reflected back again.

The final step – and the only way of knowing for certain if there is any oil – is to drill an exploration well. Even with modern technology, more than half of exploration holes fail to find commercially viable reserves of oil or gas. All this means that oil exploration is a costly business – deep water exploration wells, for example, can cost more than $100 million to drill. But the rewards are great when a good reservoir is located.

Tapping the flow

Once a reservoir has been identified and shown to be viable, it has to be prepared for production. A steel pipe (or casing) is inserted into the drill hole and made secure with cement. At first, the pressure in the reservoir is enough to send the oil spouting up the pipe to the surface, where it feeds into a structure of valves, known as a 'Christmas tree' because of its shape. This passes the oil into pipelines for storage and transport to oil refineries.

After a while, the natural pressure falls and oil companies have to resort to other techniques to recover more of the remaining oil. In earlier times, 'nodding donkey' beam pumps were used, but now a variety of other 'secondary recovery' methods have been developed, including injecting carbon dioxide or some other gas into the reservoir to increase the pressure artificially. In highly profitable oil fields, a third level of recovery – tertiary recovery – may be used, when the secondary recovery techniques are no longer sufficient. This involves reducing the oil's viscosity, usually by injecting steam, to make it easier to extract.

OIL FROM THE SEABED

THE FIRST OFFSHORE OIL WELLS WERE DRILLED AT THE TURN OF THE 20TH CENTURY. Although the process of drilling the seabed is much the same as it is for onshore wells, everything is harder and more costly due to the remoteness and the forces and pressures of working in a marine environment, where violent storms and the corrosive action of seawater damage machinery.

Offshore oil rigs can be enormous, as big as a football pitch and up to 12 storeys high. In shallower waters (down to about 500 m deep), they are usually attached to the ocean floor, standing on huge legs made of steel or concrete. These are called fixed platforms. Semi-submersible platforms are floating structures, suitable for deeper waters (down to about 900 m). Their legs are buoyant, keeping the platform afloat, but heavy enough to keep it upright. Because semi-submersible rigs are floating, they can be moved from place to place and are generally used for exploratory drilling.

Some of the larger platforms are like artificial islands. The most astonishing example is the Oil Rocks platform in the Caspian Sea off Azerbaijan. It is the world's oldest oil platform, built by the Soviet authorities in the 1940s, and still its largest, with a shifting population of some 5000 people and more than 200 km of streets. It is familiar to moviegoers from the 1999 James Bond film, *The World Is Not Enough*.

ANOTHER WORLD A North Sea rig perches perilously on stilts, as a tanker lies ready to take on board a cargo of oil. Offshore rigs are isolated, self-contained worlds set on the high seas, with their own electricity generators and desalinators to provide water.

Life on board an offshore oil rig is intense, with activity carrying on round the clock. On large fixed platforms, oil is constantly being pumped up from established wells, while drilling continues for new ones on the nearby seabed.

Mudlogging

Employees work 12-hour shifts. They include people like Mike Morley, who has been working on offshore oilrigs for 19 years, mainly in the Norwegian sector of the North Sea. He's a 'mudlogger', a geologist whose job is to predict when they are nearing oil during drilling or if a pocket of high-pressure gas is about to enter a well. He measures the drill fluid going into the borehole and makes sure that an equal volume comes out. The drill fluid is a water-based liquid – referred to as 'mud' – which is pumped to the drill bit, serving several functions including cooling the head and removing debris. If Mike sees a surging of liquid coming out, this could indicate that oil or gas is coming in and pushing the mud fluid out.

The thing that he and all oil workers fear most is a blowout, an uncontrolled flow of oil or gas up the pipe. For those on the rig, this means a potential explosion, and for the oil company it could mean the costly closure of a well. 'I measure the gas content of the mud,' says Mike. 'There is always some gas, but if I detect a big pocket it could be dangerous. The worst thing is that it could blow the drill pipe out of the hole. We'd have to abandon the rig.'

There is, however, a last line of defence if a situation like this develops. On the seabed, a huge pair of steel jaws – the blowout preventer (or BOP) – encases the drilling pipe. At the touch of a button the jaws slam shut, cutting through the pipe and sealing the hole in one swift movement. This is only done in extreme emergencies, because it could mean the end for that particular well – but it is better than being blown up.

FACTS THE WORLD'S BIGGEST OIL PRODUCERS IN 2006 WERE Saudi Arabia (514.6 million tonnes), Russia (480.5 million) and the USA (311.8 million). The biggest consumers were the USA (938.8 million tonnes), China (349.8 million) and Japan (235 million). North Americans as a whole consumed more than 3 tonnes of oil per person.

IN THE 1860s, the price of a barrel of crude oil reached the equivalent of more than US$100 in today's money – the highest ever.

SAUDI ARABIA SITS ON TOP OF NEARLY 22 PER CENT of the world's proven oil reserves. **FACTS**

One important development of recent years has been the introduction of remotely controlled drillheads. Before, each time workers wanted to drill in a different direction, they had to haul out all the pipework, place a new drill bit at the end and then feed all the pipes back down the hole again, all of which could take up half a day. Directional drilling, as it is called, means that 20 or 30 holes can emerge from a single platform, snaking under the seabed like wormholes. They can travel downslope, horizontally and even uphill, and they may be 8 km long or more.

With so many holes crossing the same area, problems can arise if a hole gets too close to a neighbouring pipeline. 'The metal in the neighbouring pipe can confuse the signals going to the drillhead and there is a danger of accidentally drilling into it,' says Mike, who saw a driller have a close shave during one of his shifts. 'We knew something was up because there were shavings of metal coming up in the drill fluid.' Luckily, the driller stopped before the neighbouring pipe was ruptured.

Shore control

Today, drilling has entered the realms of virtual reality. With sophisticated computer programmes and satellite connections, a geologist can sit at a computer on shore, wearing goggles and holding a joystick. He watches a three-dimensional image of the rock layers beneath the ground and navigates his way along the seams of rock. This allows a very high level of accuracy.

In a few years' time, it is likely that many jobs, including Mike's, will be performed onshore using computers and satellite links to the rigs. It will be more comfortable, but people like Mike may have moments of nostalgia for an environment where storms can whip up spectacular 26 m high waves or a massive sky blaze with a stunning sunset. 'Sometimes on a calm, sunny day the sea can just look amazing – completely flat as though it's frozen.'

NATURAL GAS

THE FIRST GAS USED COMMERCIALLY AS A FUEL WASN'T THE CLEAR BLUE FLAME WE KNOW TODAY – it was foul-smelling, toxic and polluting. Known as town gas, it was made by heating bituminous coal at very high temperatures in the absence of air. The resulting gas was a mixture of methane, hydrogen and carbon monoxide.

But the Earth also contains huge deposits of another kind of gas – natural gas, often found in association with oil. Of all the fossil fuels, natural gas is the one that burns most cleanly, producing less carbon dioxide and particulates than oil or coal. Yet for a long time, this abundant resource was scarcely used. When discovered, it was left where it was or burned. The problem was how to transport it. The technology to construct pipelines capable of carrying gas safely emerged only after World War II.

Today, natural gas is the fossil fuel of choice for many countries, providing 21 per cent of the world's energy consumption. In Britain, where people had been using town gas since around 1800, liquified natural gas was imported from North America

DOMED TRANSPORTER The four huge domes on BP's carrier Northwest Shearwater *contain liquified natural gas (LNG). It is being transported to receiving terminals in East Asia.*

and Algeria from the 1960s. Then, in 1966, surveys of the North Sea revealed a large natural gas deposit closer to home. By 1977, natural gas was being piped to all British homes. Worldwide, Russia holds the greatest reserves – 26 per cent of the global total.

Power in methane

Natural gas is mainly methane, but usually also contains ethane, propane, butane, carbon dioxide, nitrogen and hydrogen sulphide. During processing, these impurities – valuable byproducts in themselves – are removed. Since natural gas is colourless and odourless, gas suppliers add a strongly smelling chemical so that people will be aware of any leaks.

The main use of natural gas is in generating power – it is burned to heat water into steam that turns turbines, producing electricity. It is also widely used for heating in industrial and domestic settings and for cooking, and it is a major component in the industrial production of ammonia for use in fertilisers.

Another, increasingly popular use of natural gas is as a cleaner alternative to petrol and diesel. Two types of natural gas can be used in this way: liquified natural gas (LNG) and compressed natural gas (CNG). LNG is made by cooling gas under normal pressures to −160°C, by which point it has turned into a liquid. During the process any oxygen, carbon dioxide, sulphur compounds and water are removed, leaving 90 per cent methane. LNG has to be stored in super-insulated tanks, much like vacuum flasks, to keep it in its liquid state. CNG is simply gas that has been compressed so that it takes up less volume.

Natural gas vehicles carry the CNG or LNG in cylinders. When needed, it is released from the cylinders and travels along a pressurised pipe to the engine. Dedicated gas-fuelled vehicles

GAS SUPPLIER *Much of the natural gas used in western Europe passes along this Soviet-built pipeline, from Urengoy in north-western Siberia to Uzhhorod in western Ukraine.*

use natural gas only. Bi-fuel vehicles use natural gas for most of the time, but are able to use petrol as a reserve fuel. Dual-fuel vehicles run on diesel engines, but the diesel is used only for ignition; the bulk fuel is natural gas.

Methane hydrates: a future fuel?

A tempting prospect lies under the seabed – billions of cubic metres of methane hydrate, representing a potentially vast supply of energy. A solid composed of methane surrounded by a 'cage' of ice crystals, methane hydrate occurs naturally in two settings: in the Arctic permafrost, where cold temperatures persist in shallow sediments; and under the seabed at ocean depths of more than 300 m, where the weight of the overlying water produces high pressure. The deposits can be several hundred metres thick.

Although methane hydrate has been known about for some time, the idea of using it as a fuel is relatively recent. When gas pipelines were built through Siberia, they would occasionally clog up with a crystalline substance – a combination of water and gas – which froze at temperatures above the freezing point of water. It was methane hydrate. Then in the 1970s, sediments of it were found beneath the ocean floor.

All fuels that are burned to release their energy – wood, peat, coal, oil and gas – are rich in carbon. The carbon reacts with oxygen in the atmosphere to produce carbon dioxide, releasing energy in the process. Estimates for methane hydrates vary, but it is thought that the amount of carbon bound up in them is more than double the amount in all the conventional fossil fuels put together – enough energy for hundreds if not thousands of years.

But the recovery of the hydrates is not straightforward. They exist in difficult Arctic and deep sea environments, and methane is a greenhouse gas, ten times more damaging than carbon dioxide in warming the climate, so care is needed when disturbing the deposits. Even so, many countries are interested in this resource, and research is underway in the USA and Japan.

PERMAFROST FIELD *Traditionally the home of nomadic reindeer herders, the remote Yamal Peninsula in north-western Siberia sits above massive natural gas reserves.*

NOVYY URENGOY

THE LARGEST ONSHORE NATURAL

GAS FIELD IN THE WORLD LIES BENEATH A FROST-BITTEN CORNER OF NORTH-WESTERN SIBERIA, a place where the thermometer remains buried below freezing point for 250 days of the year and sinks to –60°C in winter. This is the harsh environment that supplies western Europe with most of its natural gas.

The Urengoy field was discovered in 1966 and Novyy Urengoy (New Urengoy), now a thriving city of 110 000 people, was founded while it was being explored. In 1984, a 4500 km gas pipeline was built connecting Urengoy with Uzhhorod in Ukraine, near the border with Slovakia. Each year Urengoygazprom, a subsidiary of the Russian gas giant OAO Gazprom, extracts 260 000 million m³ of gas and 825 000 tonnes of oil from the field.

As reserves have been used up, the field has been drilled ever deeper. The latest venture, a joint Russian-German project, uses specialised techniques to drill through frozen tundra to a depth of nearly 4 km, sometimes at an angle of 80 degrees. Drilling for the first production well started in June 2006. The new wells are expected to produce 200 billion m³ of natural gas over the next 40 years.

LOCATION Yamalo-Nenetskiy Autonomous Okrug (district) of north-western Siberia

AGE OF DEPOSIT 90–140 million years

AREA OF GAS FIELD 250 x 60 km

DEPTH 1200–3700 m

RESERVE 7.6 trillion m³ of natural gas

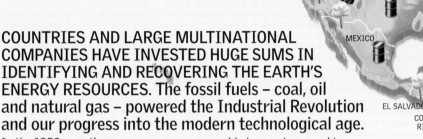

![]	MAJOR OIL FIELD
![]	MAJOR NATURAL GAS FIELD
![]	MAJOR COAL FIELD
![]	URANIUM MINE
![]	GEOTHERMAL PLANT

COUNTRIES AND LARGE MULTINATIONAL COMPANIES HAVE INVESTED HUGE SUMS IN IDENTIFYING AND RECOVERING THE EARTH'S ENERGY RESOURCES. The fossil fuels – coal, oil and natural gas – powered the Industrial Revolution and our progress into the modern technological age.

In the 1950s, another energy resource was added – uranium, used to generate nuclear power (see pages 48-49). But these resources, although abundant, are in limited supply. Once we have used them up, there will be no more. Other sources of energy are available, which are renewable – they won't run out. These include geothermal energy (see pages 42-45).

This map shows the locations of the world's major coal, oil and natural gas fields, uranium mines and geothermal plants. The tables show the top ten countries with the largest reserves of coal, oil, natural gas and uranium and the largest installed capacity for generating electricity using geothermal energy.

ENERGY RESOURCES

OIL PROVEN RESERVES, 2005

COUNTRY	RESERVES (billion barrels)
1 Saudi Arabia	264.2
2 Iran	137.5
3 Iraq	115.0
4 Kuwait	101.5
5 United Arab Emirates	97.8
6 Venezuela	79.7
7 Russia	74.4
8 Kazakhstan	39.6
9 Libya	39.1
10 Nigeria	35.9

NATURAL GAS
PROVEN RESERVES, 2005

COUNTRY	RESERVES (trillion m³)
1 Russia	47.82
2 Iran	26.74
3 Qatar	25.78
4 Saudi Arabia	6.90
5 United Arab Emirates	6.04
6 USA	5.45
7 Nigeria	5.23
8 Algeria	4.58
9 Venezuela	4.32
10 Kazakhstan	3.00

☙ COAL
PROVEN RESERVES, 2005

COUNTRY	RESERVES (million tonnes)
1 USA	246 643
2 Russia	157 010
3 China	114 500
4 India	92 445
5 South Africa	48 750
6 Ukraine	34 153
7 Kazakhstan	31 279
8 Poland	14 000
9 Brazil	10 113
10 Germany	6739

⬙ URANIUM ASSURED
RESOURCES RECOVERABLE AT A COST OF LESS THAN US$130 PER KG, 2005

COUNTRY	RESERVES (tonnes)
1 Australia	747 000
2 Kazakhstan	513 897
3 Canada	345 200
4 USA	342 000
5 South Africa	255 593
6 Namibia	182 556
7 Niger	180 466
8 Brazil	157 700
9 Russia	131 750
10 Uzbekistan	76 936

☘ GEOTHERMAL
INSTALLED CAPACITY TO PRODUCE ELECTRICITY BY MEGAWATTS ELECTRICAL (MWe), 2005

COUNTRY	POWER (MWe)
1 USA	2544
2 Philippines	1931
3 Mexico	953
4 Indonesia	797
5 Italy	790
6 Japan	535
7 New Zealand	435
8 Iceland	322
9 Costa Rica	163
10 El Salvador	151

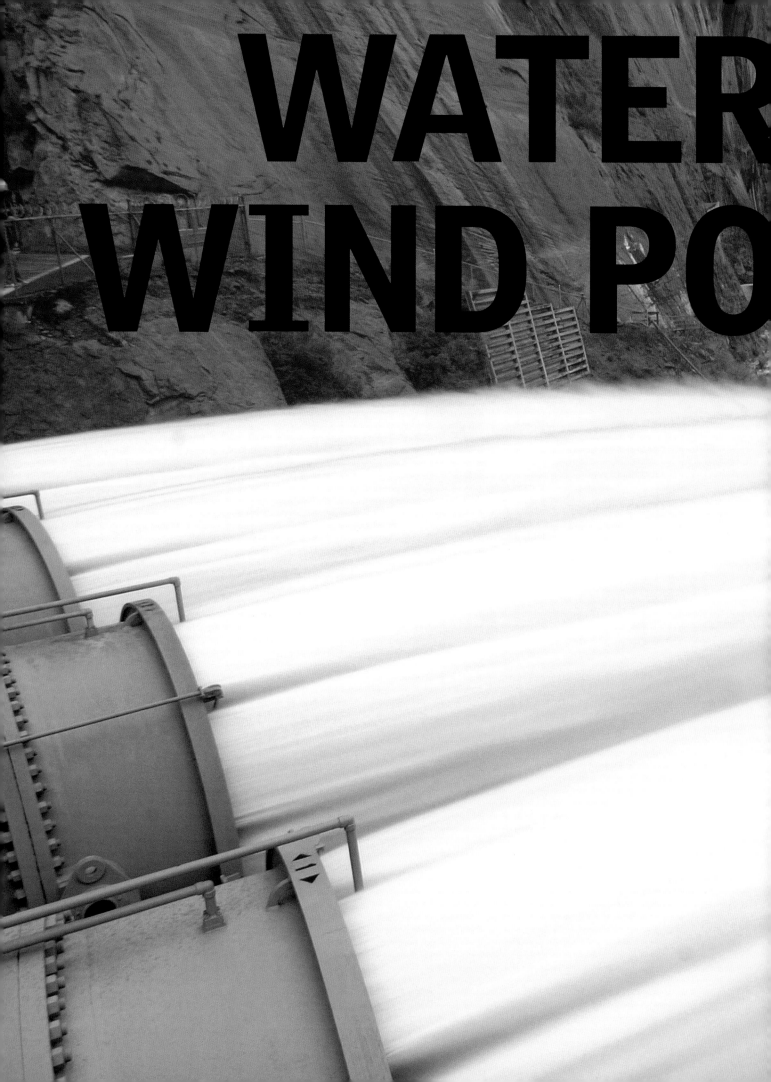

WATER
WIND PO

AND
WER

4

JETS OF WATER SHOOT INTO ARIZONA'S
GRAND CANYON at a colossal rate of 1160 m³
per second during a 2004 experiment to move
sediment down the Colorado River to restore
beaches and reclaim river habitats. It is just one
example of the way in which the power of water
can be harnessed. Elsewhere, water is used to
generate electricity. The Three Gorges Dam on
the Chang Jiang (Yangtze River) in China, is one
of several massive hydroelectric projects under
way. When fully operational, in 2009, its 32
turbines will have a capacity of around 22 500
megawatts and provide 3 per cent of China's
energy supply. It is thought that the 600 km
reservoir will be visible from the Moon. Wind
power has long been harnessed to pump water
or grind corn. Today, wind turbines generate
electricity – currently more than 74 000
megawatts globally per year and rising.

WATER AS A RESOURCE

WHEN VIEWED FROM SPACE, THE EARTH IS CLEARLY A BLUE PLANET, WHERE WATER ABOUNDS. Water covers 70 per cent of its surface – we mostly see it in the oceans, but also in rivers, ponds, lakes and reservoirs.

But although we have plenty of it – some 1.4 billion km³ in total – the most important type of water for our health and survival is in limited supply: fresh, clean drinking water. Most of the planet's water (97 per cent) is held in the oceans, leaving only 3 per cent as fresh water. With glaciers locking up about 2 per cent as ice, it leaves only 1 per cent in ground water, lakes, rivers and the atmosphere. We have to manage this most precious of resources with extreme care.

Today, around 1 billion people do not have access to clean water, while 3 billion do not have adequate sanitation. Partly, this is a result of geography. Climate differences mean that freshwater supplies are unequally distributed around the globe – in hot, arid climates, water is naturally more scarce than in more temperate climates. Political, cultural and demographic influences also play a part: when a lot of people share a limited supply of water, inevitably some will lose out. Poverty is another factor, governing the amount of water people can afford to use and how easy it is to access.

The daily hunt for water

In the developing world, people may face a daily trek of several kilometres to fetch fresh water – in Africa, this task is traditionally assigned to women. Lucy Akanboguure from Ghana describes her daily routine before a charity helped her community to gain easier access to clean water. 'I had to get up at 3 am every day to walk 5 km to collect water from a river. I did not arrive back before 10 am, which meant I was often late for work at the local school where I was teacher. ... Fetching water took up most of the women's day.' Things changed dramatically after the charity WaterAid helped Lucy's community to install wells and hand pumps. 'On the first day after the hand pump was installed I woke up at 6 am and cried out because I was too late to fetch water from the river. Then I realised that my excited children had woken earlier and filled the water pots with clean water ... I feel so happy having water at my doorstep, 24 hours a day, knowing that my children are safe from water-related diseases.'

My excited children had woken earlier and filled the water pots with clean water ... I feel so happy having water at my doorstep, 24 hours a day, knowing that my children are safe from water-related diseases.

THE WATER ROUND Women collect water at a borehole near Doropo in northern Côte d'Ivoire. In Africa, boreholes with manual pumps are gradually replacing traditional village wells. The water from the boreholes is cleaner than that of traditional wells, 70 per cent of which is unfit for drinking. Also, containers made of plastic, enamelled metal or aluminium are replacing canaris (large terracotta jugs) and gourds for carrying the precious resource.

FACTS

ILLNESSES FROM INSANITARY WATER ARE THE MAJOR

cause of infant mortality in developing nations, although rates are now falling. Diarrhoea, for example, kills more than 1.5 million children worldwide before the age of five. As populations grow in Africa and Asia, providing better access to clean drinking water is a major challenge.

IN SUB-SAHARAN

Africa people make do with an average of 10 litres of fresh water a day. The average American uses 350 litres.

EVERYBODY

SHOULD HAVE ACCESS TO AT LEAST 50 LITRES of fresh water a day, according to UN recommendations.

FACTS

THE WATERY PLANET

IMAGINE A CUBE-SHAPED TANK OF WATER WHOSE SIDES ARE ALL 10 KM LONG. That is the amount of water the Sun's heat evaporates from the oceans every day. It is part of the hydrological cycle, a huge circulating flow in which water is constantly being moved from the oceans to the atmosphere to the land and back to the oceans again.

Rain and snow (collectively called precipitation) are part of the hydrological cycle, and they are the source of fresh water. Most precipitation falls over the oceans. Of the portion that falls to the ground, some is evaporated back up again into the atmosphere, and some sinks into the ground. Some, too, gets frozen to form icecaps and glaciers. In the ground, the roots of plants take up some of the water and transpire it into the atmosphere, while the rest drains into streams and rivers or gathers in aquifers (underground reservoirs).

Water underground

There is a hundred times more fresh water underground than in all the world's rivers, lakes and reservoirs put together – although not all of it is clean enough to be usable and some of it is difficult to reach. Water close to the surface is seen in boggy land and marshes. But much ground water lies hundreds of metres deep. It seeps downwards through the soil, moving through the spaces between soil and rock particles, until it reaches a layer of rock that it is saturated (it can't hold any more water). This is called the water table. Different types of rock can hold different amounts of water. Granite is not very porous, while sandstone and gravel are porous and so make good aquifers. We can obtain water by drilling a well down to the water table. In artesian wells, the water rises from the aquifer under its own pressure; in other kinds of wells, the water has to be pumped up.

PRECIPITATION Droplets of condensed water in the clouds fall to the surface of the Earth as rain or snow (precipitation). On average, a total of about 500 000 km³ of water drops from the sky as precipitation each year, of which the vast majority – nearly 79 per cent – falls over the oceans.

THE HYDROLOGICAL CYCLE
The Sun provides the energy that drives the hydrological cycle, evaporating water from the oceans and circulating the atmosphere. The evaporated water forms clouds, gets moved by wind and in due course precipitates out as rain or snow. Eventually, the water precipitated over land makes its way back to the oceans.

EVAPORATION

PRECIPITATION

EVAPORATION Ocean water, heated by the Sun, evaporates into the air as vapour. The vapour cools as it rises and condenses into clouds, which are spread around the globe. Other, much smaller sources of water vapour in the atmosphere include water that is transpired from plants and water evaporated directly from the ground.

DRAINAGE Of the precipitation that falls over land, some drains into streams and rivers and so makes its way back to the oceans. Some seeps into the soil as ground water, of which a proportion sinks into underground reservoirs called aquifers. Water may also travel through underground caves and may re-emerge at the surface as freshwater springs.

DRAINAGE

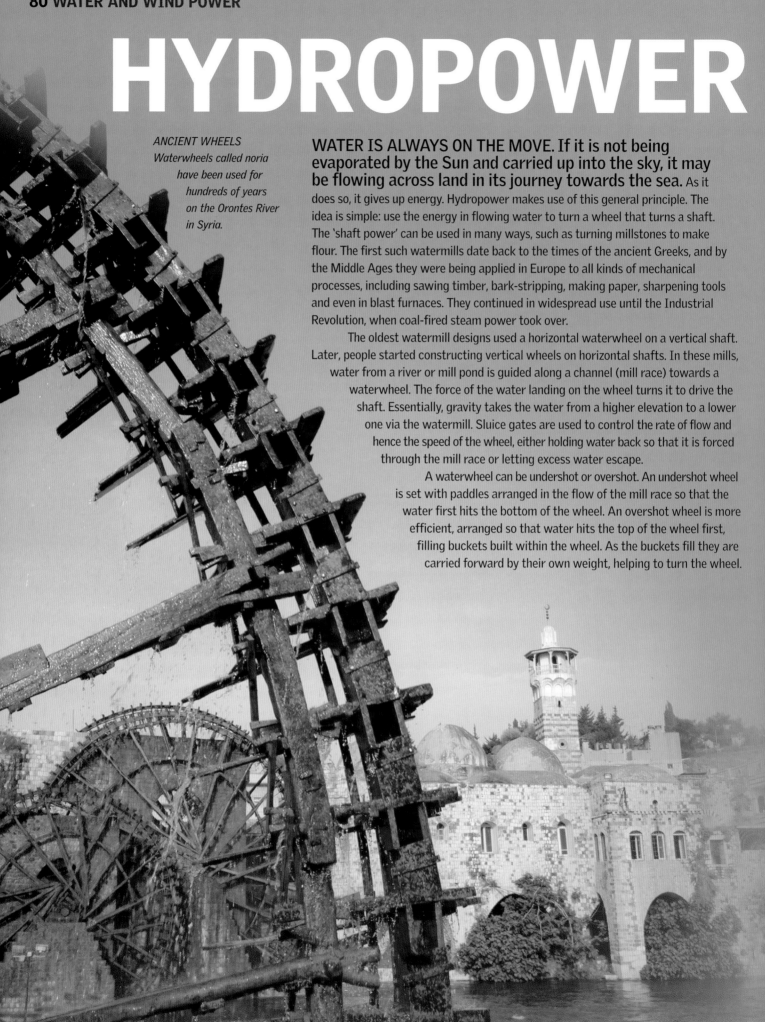

HYDROPOWER

ANCIENT WHEELS
Waterwheels called noria
have been used for
hundreds of years
on the Orontes River
in Syria.

WATER IS ALWAYS ON THE MOVE. If it is not being evaporated by the Sun and carried up into the sky, it may be flowing across land in its journey towards the sea. As it does so, it gives up energy. Hydropower makes use of this general principle. The idea is simple: use the energy in flowing water to turn a wheel that turns a shaft. The 'shaft power' can be used in many ways, such as turning millstones to make flour. The first such watermills date back to the times of the ancient Greeks, and by the Middle Ages they were being applied in Europe to all kinds of mechanical processes, including sawing timber, bark-stripping, making paper, sharpening tools and even in blast furnaces. They continued in widespread use until the Industrial Revolution, when coal-fired steam power took over.

The oldest watermill designs used a horizontal waterwheel on a vertical shaft. Later, people started constructing vertical wheels on horizontal shafts. In these mills, water from a river or mill pond is guided along a channel (mill race) towards a waterwheel. The force of the water landing on the wheel turns it to drive the shaft. Essentially, gravity takes the water from a higher elevation to a lower one via the watermill. Sluice gates are used to control the rate of flow and hence the speed of the wheel, either holding water back so that it is forced through the mill race or letting excess water escape.

A waterwheel can be undershot or overshot. An undershot wheel is set with paddles arranged in the flow of the mill race so that the water first hits the bottom of the wheel. An overshot wheel is more efficient, arranged so that water hits the top of the wheel first, filling buckets built within the wheel. As the buckets fill they are carried forward by their own weight, helping to turn the wheel.

Electricity by water power

Watermills had become very efficient by the 19th century, but they always had the disadvantage that any industry using the power produced by a watermill had to be positioned close to water. Coal-fired steam power gave manufacturers the freedom to set up more or less wherever was convenient for them. Later on in the century, a new use was found for water power – to generate electricity in hydroelectric plants. Today, this is the most important function of hydropower.

Any large river that has a significant fall in elevation can be used to generate electricity. Most of the world's large rivers now have hydroelectric dams across them, including the Columbia, Congo, Danube, Ganges, Indus, Paraná, Niger, Nile and Zambezi. The dam blocks the flow of the river, storing up the water behind it in a reservoir. Near the base of the dam wall are several intake valves. Each one allows water to flow through a channel, called the penstock, that leads towards a turbine (basically, a type of waterwheel). The moving water turns the turbine, which is connected by a shaft to a generator, which produces electricity.

The intake of water can be controlled as and when required to generate power. After passing through the turbine, the water flows through to the other side of the dam and carries on down the river. Powerlines carry the electricity from the generator to wherever it is needed.

Hydroelectrical potential

The Victorian industrialist and inventor, William Armstrong, was one of the first people to spot the possibility of using hydropower to generate electricity. In 1870, he built what was probably the world's first hydroelectric plant on his country estate, Cragside, in Northumberland, England. As its name suggests, the house stands on a craggy hillside. Armstrong first of all used a hydraulic engine to power various pieces of household gadgetry, including a lift, a rotating spit in the kitchen and machinery for washing laundry. Then he harnessed water from a lake on the estate to drive a dynamo for generating electricity. Over the years, he expanded the scheme until he was using hydropower to provide electricity for the house and many farm buildings.

Nowadays, hydropower is the most widely used form of renewable energy, accounting for around 16 per cent of the world's electricity production. In some countries, the natural geology and climate mean that it contributes much more than the world average. In Norway, for example, a land of deep fjords, snow-capped mountains and heavy rainfall, hydroenergy is abundant, and 850 hydropower plants supply more than 99 per cent of the country's electricity. This puts Norway in an extremely advantageous position. It also has large reserves of oil and natural gas but does not need to use them to generate electricity. Instead, it sells most of its oil and gas to western Europe, making it the world's third largest oil exporter, after Saudi Arabia and Russia.

Although hydropower only works in regions where there is a suitable river with an appropriate flow and drop of elevation, there is still enormous potential for development. Worldwide, we are currently using no more than about a third of the planet's hydropower potential. According to the World Energy Council,

THE WORLD'S LARGEST WATERFALLS

Nowhere is the energy in water more spectacularly evident than in waterfalls. Some of the world's largest falls are listed here by the volume of water pouring over them.

WATERFALL	RIVER	VOLUME (m³/second)	
Inga Falls, Democratic Republic of Congo	Congo	42 476	The world's largest waterfalls, over about 14.5 km of the Congo
Khone Falls, Laos	Mekong	11 610	Asia's largest falls
Niagara Falls, USA/Canada	Niagara	2410	North America's largest falls
Iguaçu Falls, Brazil/Argentina	Iguazu	1746	South America's largest falls
Victoria Falls, Zambia/Zimbabwe also called Mosi-oa-Tunya ('The Smoke that Thunders')	Zambezi	975	At 108 m high and 1700 m wide, they form the world's largest sheet of falling water
Rhine Falls, Switzerland	Rhine	370	Europe's largest falls

NIAGARA FALLS The Horseshoe Falls (below) are one of three that make up the Niagara Falls. Some of their power is used to generate electricity for parts of Ontario and New York State.

ITAIPU DAM

THE MOST POWERFUL HYDROELECTRIC PLANT IN
THE WORLD IS HOUSED IN THE ITAIPÚ DAM. Straddling the Paraguay/
Brazil border, the dam constrains the might of the Paraná River, turning its force
into an excess of 90 million megawatt hours per year, enough to supply the
sprawling cities of São Paulo and Rio de Janeiro with most of their electricity
needs. Itaipu provides almost 30 per cent of Brazil's
electricity consumption and 90 per cent of Paraguay's.
By March 2007 there were 20 turbine units in place,
bringing the plant's capacity up to 14 000 megawatts.

    Construction of the dam, which began in 1975 as a
joint project between Brazil and Paraguay, was a herculean
feat. It took almost three years for workers to dig a 2 km
diversion channel for the Paraná, excavating 50 million
tonnes of earth and rock in the process. The dam itself
contains enough concrete to make five Hoover Dams and
enough iron and steel to construct 380 Eiffel Towers. The
main part of the dam is made of hollow concrete blocks and
stands about 714 m wide and 196 m tall. In 1994, the Itaipú
Dam was voted one of the Seven Wonders of the Modern
World in a global survey conducted by the American Society
of Civil Engineers.

    In order to minimise the dam's impact on the environment,
more than 27 000 animals were caught, moved and released
elsewhere, and 11 000 plants transplanted before the flooding
of the dam. Areas of deforestation were also replanted.

LOCATION: Brazil and Paraguay
CAPACITY (2007): 14 000 megawatts
COST: US$ 18 billion
TURBINE UNITS: 20
MOST ENERGY PRODUCED: 93 million
    megawatt hours in 2000
AVERAGE FLOW OF PARANÁ RIVER:
    10 000 m³ per second
RESERVOIR CAPACITY: 2.9×10^{10} m³

VITAL STATISTICS

hydropower could be used in 150 countries and is particularly underutilised in developing countries, where energy is needed most.

Many experts, however, have concerns about hydropower. It is generally considered to be a clean and renewable source of energy, with lower operating costs and a longer plant life than other large-scale power-generating installations. But there is a problem with the positioning of large hydroschemes. Building a dam has consequences for the surrounding environment. Creating a reservoir may flood large areas of land and infrastructure, leading to loss and in some cases extinction of local wildlife, resettlement issues for local people and the drowning of historic or natural landscapes. Other local effects of enormous dams include increased levels of fog and humidity and earth tremors due to the weight of the water. In addition, the proliferation of water weeds in the reservoir can encourage the spread of waterborne diseases.

One of the most spectacular projects is the massive Three Gorges Dam on the Chang Jiang (Yangtze River) in China. Due to become fully operational in 2009, it will have 32 generators, with a total capacity of 22 500 megawatts, enough to provide electricity for about 20 million households. But the social and environmental costs are huge. The reservoir, which will eventually stretch for 600 km from end to end, has already displaced more than a million people, and tens of thousands more will lose their homes and land by the time it is finished. A number of unique archaeological sites will disappear beneath its waters, and at least two endangered animal species, the Chinese paddlefish and the Siberian crane, will lose habitat.

How clean?

The effects of hydroelectric schemes are felt downriver, too. There may be scouring (erosion) of riverbeds, because the water leaving a dam has few sediments. Water is generally cooler once it leaves a dam, and this can disrupt fish living downriver. Also, the dam may obstruct fish migration.

On top of all this, there is growing concern among experts that far from being a clean source of renewable energy, large-scale hydropower plants may actually be contributing to global warming in much the same way that power stations using fossil fuels do. The problem lies with the vast reservoirs of water held in by the dams. Any dead organic matter in the water sinks to the bottom of a reservoir, and in tropical regions, in particular, this organic matter can produce vast amounts of methane, which is a more potent greenhouse gas even than carbon dioxide. It has been estimated that reservoirs supplying hydropower plants in

ASWAN HIGH DAM
Completed in 1970, Egypt's Aswan High Dam has lived up to many of its builders' hopes. It has allowed countless villages across Egypt to enjoy the benefits of electricity, while its reservoir, Lake Nasser, captures the waters of the Nile's annual flood so that they can be released during the dry season. But it has also had disruptive effects. It displaced 90 000 people, and archaeological sites had to be moved, such as the temples of Abu Simbel, rebuilt in an artificial hill by Lake Nasser (right). Also, regions downstream have suffered from the loss of fertile silt swept down by the floodwaters. Farmers have to use artificial fertilisers, leading to chemical pollution, and without the silt, there have been problems of erosion in the Nile Delta.

tropical and subtropical locations can produce more greenhouse gases per kilowatt/hour of energy generated than burning the equivalent amount of fossil fuels.

Microhydro power

The problems associated with large-scale hydroprojects are focusing attention on smaller, more localised hydropower schemes. Microhydro systems are normally built as 'run of the river' projects, which means that they use the natural downward flow of a river and collect the kinetic energy in the water. Water is diverted from a high point and fed down a pipe and through a turbine. The water then travels onwards to return to the river. Several small-scale systems can run off a river and since the water flows back into the river, the flow is not reduced for people living downstream.

Definitions vary, but a microhydro system typically produces less than 100 kilowatts. Since water is constantly flowing, there is no need to store the energy in batteries, as it is always available. The systems are cheap to install and run, which makes them good for developing countries. They are also becoming popular elsewhere, as people become more environmentally aware.

Before installing a microhydro system, a basic calculation must be done to see if it can generate enough energy. Multiply the 'head' of water (the vertical drop) in metres by the flow in litres per second – this can be gauged by estimating the cross-sectional area of a part of the stream, then using a float to measure the rate at which the water flows between that and another point along the stream. Multiply this figure by ten to account for the acceleration due to gravity, and divide the answer by two (to account for inefficiencies in the system) and the answer gives an idea of power in watts. A turbine installed on a hill stream with a head of 15 m and a flow of 15 litres per second will generate just over 1 kilowatt, enough for the basic needs of one household.

HOOVER DAM

'I CAME, I SAW AND I WAS CONQUERED.' PRESIDENT FRANKLIN D. ROOSEVELT'S WORDS AT THE DEDICATION OF THE HOOVER DAM on September 30, 1935, summed up the impact of the towering curved wall of concrete holding back the waters of Lake Mead. The dam, which sits across the Black Canyon on the border of Arizona and Nevada, broke many records when it was built: at 221 m tall and 201 m thick at its base, it was the world's largest concrete structure, and it had the biggest turbines and the most powerful generators. Lake Mead, the 185 km long reservoir created behind the dam, is the largest man-made lake in the United States, holding approximately 35.2 km³ of water. By the time it reaches the dam's turbines, water from Lake Mead is flowing at a speed of around 137 km/h.

The dam was built to tame the Colorado River, a tempestuous flood in winter which dried up to a trickle in summer. It would enable better irrigation of farmland and provide southern California with a dependable water supply, as well as generating electricity. Today, the dam's 17 turbines, with a combined capacity of 2000 megawatts, supply Las Vegas and much of Nevada, Arizona and California with electricity. During peak periods of demand enough water flows through the dam's generators to fill 15 average-size swimming pools in one second.

DESERT CITY Hoover Dam generates electricity and supplies municipal and industrial water for the ever-expanding city of Las Vegas.

AERIAL VIEWS Hoover Dam (left) was named after President Herbert Hoover, who was instrumental in getting the project off the ground. Hoover Dam (small circle, below) and the sprawl of Las Vegas 48 km to its west (large circle) are shown on this satellite photograph of the area.

A technical wonder

The project, which began in 1931, was a monumental feat of engineering, made all the more remarkable because it was carried out during a time of severe economic depression. At one point there were 5000 men working on the dam and temporary communities such as Ragtown sprang up around Black Canyon.

In order to divert the Colorado River while the dam was built and the concrete poured, four 17 m wide diversion tunnels were excavated through the canyon walls, two on the Nevada side and two on the Arizona side. Each tunnel was lined with a 90 cm thick coating of concrete. For five years the river flowed through these diversion tunnels while construction of the dam progressed on the dry canyon bottom.

The dam itself required three million cubic metres of concrete. Engineers estimated that under normal circumstances it would take around 125 years for this amount of concrete to

cool down if it was poured in one continuous block. To get round this problem the dam was built in a series of interlocking columns. To speed up the cooling process, freezing cold water was pumped through coiled pipes into the wet concrete. As each block cooled, the water pipes were cut off and filled with grout.

The original plans for a plain, functional-looking concrete façade were deemed too low key for such a ground-breaking project. Instead, architect Gordon B. Kaufmann was commissioned to create a striking Art Deco design, complete with sculptured turrets. Today, the magnificent complex stands as a testament to the builders who, within five years, had managed to tame the Colorado River.

By the time it reaches the dam's turbines, water from Lake Mead is flowing at a speed of around 137 km/h.

THE GRAVITATIONAL PULL OF THE MOON IS THE ULTIMATE SOURCE OF TIDAL POWER. Other forms of hydropower harvest the Sun's energy after it has shifted water through part of the hydrological cycle. Tidal power relies on the force of the Moon, as it drives the ebb and flow of tides. These happen because the Moon's gravitational pull makes our oceans bulge outwards towards it, with a corresponding bulge on the side of the Earth opposite the Moon. As the Earth makes its daily rotation, the two bulges sweep across its surface as tides. There is nothing new about using tides to provide energy. During the Middle Ages, people built tidal mills in France, England and the Orkney islands; tidal flows turned waterwheels that drove millstones for grinding cereals. Then, in the 20th century, scientists again started investigating the tides as a source of energy.

Barrages and turbines

The first method they developed involves building barrages to trap the sea at high tide. A barrier is built across a bay or estuary with a tidal range of at least 5 m, and as the sea flows from one side of the barrage to the other its energy is harnessed to produce electricity. In ebb generation, the most popular method, an incoming tide flows through sluices in the barrage. At high tide the sluices are shut, holding the water back. As the

There is nothing new about using tidal power to provide energy. During the Middle Ages, people built tidal mills in France, England and the Orkney islands. Tidal flows turned waterwheels that drove millstones for grinding cereals.

TIDAL POWER

tide goes out, there is a difference in levels between the receding tide and the water held behind the barrage. When the difference, or 'head', is at least half the tidal range, the captured water is allowed to flow through turbines, generating electricity. France operates the world's most powerful tidal barrage power plant in the Rance estuary in Brittany, with a capacity of 240 megawatts.

There are problems with tidal barrages, however. They generate electricity only at certain points in the tidal cycle, making it difficult to respond to sudden demands for energy. They are also costly to build, and they can have a negative impact on delicate coastal ecosystems. Because of this, the current focus of research is on tapping the kinetic energy in fast-flowing tidal currents, rather like a wind turbine uses the energy in wind. This has the advantage that plants can be placed in ocean currents farther from the shore.

Several tidal technologies are being researched. In the 1990s, tidal current power was tested in Loch Linnhe, Scotland, using a turbine held in place by cables. Another system, SeaFlow, off Lynmouth in North Devon, makes use of the strong currents in the Bristol Channel. Yet another device being tested, called Stingray, uses a flapping hydroplane that oscillates in the flowing sea current, working a piston up and down to drive a generator.

EBB GENERATION The tidal barrage plant in the Rance estuary (left and below) has been operating since 1966.

UNDERWATER WINDMILL A tidal farm, such as this one due to open off the Anglesey coast, North Wales, in 2010, uses water currents and tides to generate electricity.

WAVE POWER

WAVE POWER IS A MANIFESTATION OF SOLAR ENERGY. The Sun generates winds, which transfer some of their energy to the oceans as they push up the surface into waves. Most waves are generated between latitudes of 30–60° North and South, so regions in the northern and southern temperate zones have the most potential for harnessing wave power. As waves reach shallower waters they lose energy, but variations in the topography of the seabed can focus wave energy, producing localised concentrations near the shore.

The first wave-power systems were built onshore, but as wave motion is greatest at the ocean surface, most devices now aim to capture it offshore. There is potentially more energy available from wave power than from tidal energy as it can be exploited in many more areas. Because it can be sited off the coast, it has less environmental impact, too. Wave energy is costly: devices must harness energy efficiently and be robust enough to withstand stormy seas and corrosion from saltwater. Once these problems are overcome, it offers a potentially limitless energy resource for countries with long coastlines.

ENERGY FROM THE SEA The world's first commercial wave-power station opened in 2000 on Islay in Scotland. It uses the oscillating water column system to generate electricity for around 400 homes. Electricity from the station is also used to recharge the island's electric bus.

Waves into power

The first commercial wave-power plant uses breaking waves to operate a system known as an oscillating water column (OWC). As an incoming wave enters a partially submerged chamber, air in the chamber is compressed and pushed upwards through a hole leading to a turbine. The rush of air drives the turbine, generating electricity. As the wave recedes and sucks air out, the turbine runs again.

The power in a wave reduces as it reaches the shore because energy is absorbed by the seabed, so a range of offshore energy-capturing devices are being developed.

AN OSCILLATING WATER COLUMN

As a wave breaks on the shoreline (1), seawater enters the wave capture chamber and raises the water level (2). The rising water pushes air in the chamber upwards and through a hole at the top (3). The rush of air turns the turbine's blades (4). As air is sucked out by the receding wave, the turbine turns again.

The first to be used commercially is called Pelamis. It was developed by Scottish firm Ocean Power Delivery and is named after a type of watersnake, reflecting the way the device moves. Each 120 m unit is made up of four huge steel tubes, each one the size of a train carriage, joined end to end by hinges. Several rows of parallel units can be used, increasing the amount of energy harvested. A 30-megawatt wave farm would consist of about 40 units occupying around 1 km² of ocean.

The device is designed to work in depths of about 50 m. Tethered to the seabed, units float on the surface pointing into the oncoming waves. Max Carcas from Ocean Power Delivery explained how it works. '[It's] a bit like a ship at anchor or a flag on a flagpole, it self-orientates into the waves. Waves travel down the length of the machine and in doing so each of the sections, each of these train carriages, move up and down and side to side.' Hydraulic hinges connecting the segments resist the motion, driving a generator. The electricity is transferred down cables to the seabed and then to the shore. In 2006, Portugal began installing the £6 million system off the town of Peniche on the Atlantic coast. Eventually, the project will deliver 2.25 megawatts of energy – enough to power 1500 households.

Buoys, swings and dragons

Other systems that generate energy by bobbing up and down at or beneath the water surface are under development. Like Pelamis, the McCabe Wave Pump generates electricity using hinges between floating sections, in this case three rectangular steel pontoons. The central section stays relatively still and the sections on either side move up and down in relation to it. The energy is captured by hydraulic pumps in the hinges.

The Archimedes Wave Swing consists of a large, cylinder-shaped buoy fixed to the seabed. Waves move an outer, air-filled casing – the 'floater' – up and down against the lower, fixed cylinder and the movement turns a generator shaft. The PowerBuoy floats at the surface. As the buoy moves with the waves a piston-like structure inside it moves and drives a generator. The AquaBuOY has a tube beneath it that is open to the sea at both ends and contains a piston connected to a hosepump. The movement of the bobbing buoy relative to the piston sucks in water and pushes it through a turbine.

The Wave Dragon is a type of floating reservoir. A pair of large, curved floating arms gather waves into the reservoir, and water escapes through the bottom via low-head turbines.

WAVE MACHINE A Pelamis unit in the Orkneys, Scotland, snakes across the water surface, flexing in the oncoming waves.

HARNESSING THE POWER OF THE WIND IS AN ANCIENT PHENOMENON. For centuries, windmills have been a distinctive feature of many landscapes, producing energy to pump water or to grind corn. Instead of the wooden shutters and fabric sails of the traditional windmills, today's new generation of wind turbines have two or usually three sleek, rotating

According to the World Energy Council, the potential wind resource globally is several times greater than the current global demand.

WIND
POWER

blades that convert the energy in the wind into electricity. They operate on a simple principle. When wind turns the propellor-like blades, they spin a shaft which connects to a generator. The larger turbines – with enormous blades often around 40 m long – are mounted at the top of a tall tower in order to utilise faster wind speeds. These turbines are grouped together on wind farms, which are connected to the electrical grid. The largest model, *Enercon E112*, is 186 m tall and capable of generating 6 megawatts of power.

Mini wind turbines – typically generating 2 kilowatts of electricity – provide power for households in remote, off-grid locations. However, as wind energy is intermittent, the turbines are used to charge up batteries so that power is stored until required. In urban areas, micro wind turbines, which can be installed on the top of buildings, have an output of 400 watts – enough to run four 100-watt lightbulbs.

The right site

Engineers carefully monitor an area for a prospective wind farm, drawing up detailed wind maps. One of the main requirements is a site with a constant flow of wind that isn't too turbulent. The wind speed should be at least 18 km per hour, or 5 m per second. Turbines are inefficient at temperatures below −20°C and they shut down during very high winds of around 80 km an hour, or 15 m per second.

Wind farms may be sited onshore, offshore or near-shore. Onshore wind farms tend to be located on ridgelines several kilometres inland from the shore. This is in order to exploit the wind's acceleration as it is forced up over the ridge. Offshore wind farms explore the generally faster wind speeds over the sea. These turbines, which are positioned 10 km or more offshore, are less obtrusive than those on land but are more expensive to install and maintain. Wind farms on or near the shore take advantage of land–sea breezes, but their siting in environmentally sensitive coastal areas can cause controversy.

Energy for the future

There are many advantages to wind power. There are no harmful emissions and the land beneath the structures can still usually be used for farming. And because the wind will always keep blowing, this is a renewable energy source. Other advantages include minimal fuel costs and relatively low-maintenance costs. And wind turbines can be taken down with minimal damage to the environment.

Although worldwide wind power generation quadrupled between 2000 and 2006, it still supplies only 1 per cent of the world's electrical power. According to the World Energy Council, however, the potential wind resource globally is several times greater than the current global demand. In Denmark, where the government has been encouraging this alternative energy source for several decades, wind power accounts for 20 per cent of electricity use, the highest percentage of any country. In fact, Europe leads the way in wind power, contributing two-thirds of the globally installed capacity. At the end of 2006, Germany alone produced 20 622 megawatts of electricty through wind power, accounting for nearly 28 per cent of the global share. Second is Spain, generating 11 615 megawatts and with a global share of 15.6 per cent. The main factors contributing to Europe's lead is a good wind resource, a high electricity demand and a political incentive to promote alternative energies. In some countries there are plentiful wind resources, but no demand for electricity, such as sparsely populated Patagonia in Argentina.

TRADITIONAL POWER SOURCE
Restored windmills dot the hillside
outside the town of Consuegra in
central Spain. Built in the 16th century,
they were used for grinding flour.

RICH
AND RARE

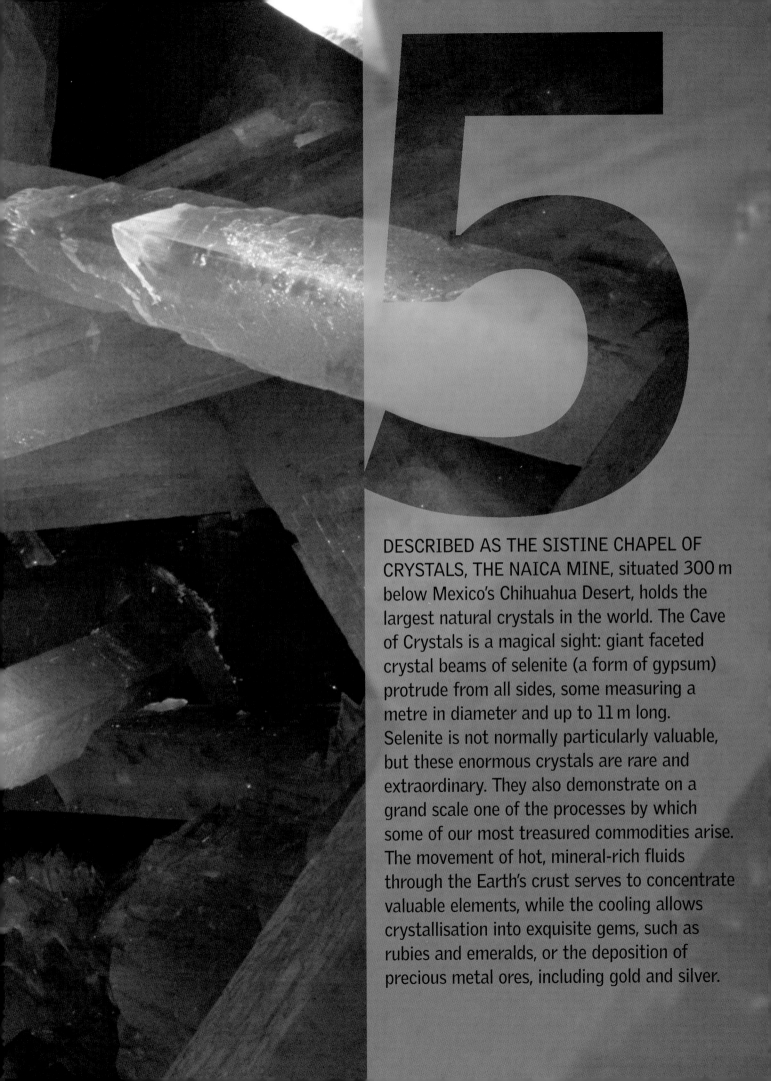

5

DESCRIBED AS THE SISTINE CHAPEL OF CRYSTALS, THE NAICA MINE, situated 300 m below Mexico's Chihuahua Desert, holds the largest natural crystals in the world. The Cave of Crystals is a magical sight: giant faceted crystal beams of selenite (a form of gypsum) protrude from all sides, some measuring a metre in diameter and up to 11 m long. Selenite is not normally particularly valuable, but these enormous crystals are rare and extraordinary. They also demonstrate on a grand scale one of the processes by which some of our most treasured commodities arise. The movement of hot, mineral-rich fluids through the Earth's crust serves to concentrate valuable elements, while the cooling allows crystallisation into exquisite gems, such as rubies and emeralds, or the deposition of precious metal ores, including gold and silver.

GOLD

ANCIENT FIGURE
For the Incas, gold took on value when it was crafted into objects of beauty, such as this female figure.

IF ALL THE GOLD THAT HAS EVER BEEN MINED – SOME 158 000 TONNES – WAS TO BE CAST IN A SINGLE LUMP, IT WOULD FORM A CUBE MEASURING JUST 20 M ALONG EACH SIDE. This may seem surprisingly small, but gold is very dense – twice as dense as lead – and a little goes a long way. It is the softest, most malleable of all the metals, while its high ductile strength allows it to be stretched a long way before breaking. One troy ounce (31.1 g) of gold can be hammered into a wafer-thin sheet covering 9 m², or drawn out to make a piece of wire 100 km long and thinner than a human hair.

Gold was the first metal to be worked, probably because it occurs in its metallic, or pure, state in the Earth's crust, and because, being soft, it is easy to hammer into shape. The word gold probably comes from the Indo-European root *ghel*, which means yellow. Its chemical symbol is Au, which comes from the latin *aurum*, meaning 'glowing dawn'. Both are appropriate names for this lustrous yellow metal, and because gold is inert – that is, it does not react with most other chemicals – it stays shiny for years without tarnishing (unlike metals such as copper or silver). Its ductility, malleability, attractive appearance and relative rarity have put a high price on gold – so high that it has been fought over through the centuries, and the desire for it has led many people astray.

Pure gold is yellow, but it often occurs in natural alloys with other metals that affect its hue. It is commonly found with silver, which gives it a paler colour. When the silver content reaches 20 per cent, the alloy is known as electrum. Red or 'rose' gold may contain trace amounts of copper, while white gold may be mixed with silver, platinum, zinc or nickel. A bluish tinge occurs if gold is mixed with a little iron. Metals such as iridium, rhodium and palladium help to harden gold.

Gold, like other precious metals, is measured in troy ounces: 1 troy ounce equals 31.1 g. In medieval times there were no standard units, and the measurement may have derived from the city of Troyes in France, which was an important trading city in those days. The purity of gold is measured in carats. Pure gold has 24 carats, while 18-carat gold is three-quarters pure (the other quarter being another metal), and 12-carat gold is half pure. The fineness of gold is another expression of purity. It is measured in parts per thousand, so 750 fine is the same as 18-carat gold.

'The sweat of the Sun'

The oldest gold objects ever recovered are 6000-year-old grave goods that were placed in an ancient burial ground at Varna in modern-day Bulgaria. The golden artefacts recovered from the 280 graves show a high level of

MODERN TREASURE Gold is ideal for delicate, intricate items of jewellery. This 1960s butterfly brooch has movable wings.

Symbol of success

Although gold has been usurped by platinum as the highest-priced metal, it continues to signify luxury and prestige. The top prize in many contests is a gold medal, most famously the Olympic gold medal, which is actually gold-plated. Until 1980, the 66 mm diameter Nobel prize medals were 200 g of 23-carat gold; now they are 18-carat green gold, plated with 24-carat gold. The 34 cm tall Oscar statuettes awarded by the US Academy of Motion Picture Arts and Sciences are plated in 24-carat gold. The Palme d'Or presented at the Cannes Film Festival is solid 24-carat gold attached to a piece of cut-glass crystal. The football World Cup is a 32 cm high statue of solid 18-carat gold.

Being so soft, gold is easy to fashion into intricate shapes and designs, and has always been popular for jewellery. Around 2000 tonnes of gold are used in jewellery each year, which is almost as much as is mined. In India people traditionally wear their wealth as gold jewellery. Such is the extent of this habit that if jewellery is included with the more usual estimates of gold bullion, India holds the greatest store of gold in the world. Gold has also been spun into thread for use in textiles for royal and religious robes, and for tapestries and wedding gowns.

A thoroughly modern metal

Even if you don't realise it, you probably own a small amount of gold. Computers, mobile phones, CD players – in fact, all modern electrical appliances rely on gold components, because it is an excellent conductor of electricity. Only silver and copper are better than gold at conducting electricity, but they do not have the same resistance to corrosion.

A very fine layer of gold can be plated over a less expensive metal to make a superior electrical contact. Drawn out into fine wire, gold is used to connect silicon chips in circuit boards. Tiny amounts are all that is needed: a typical personal computer contains about 0.1 g of gold. According to the World Gold Council, about 200 tonnes of gold were used in electronics and electrical components in 2005.

---

craftsmanship and include sceptres, bracelets, pendants and earrings. Pictures on Egyptian tombs show that the ancient Egyptians were working with gold around 3000 BC, and it is thought that in China gold production probably began in the Shang Dynasty, some 4000 years ago.

The beauty and durability of gold led ancient peoples to use it for their most precious and revered objects. To the Incas, it was 'the sweat of the Sun'. They had an abundant supply of gold in placer and surface deposits. As they did not use money, gold had no financial value. Instead, they used it on buildings and for making all sorts of objects in the belief that it reflected the glory of the Sun God.

Loot

Many ancient peoples used gold as currency. But golden treasures and coins were often the first objects that invading nations seized in times of war, and the headdresses, jewellery, figures, goblets, coins and other gold items would be melted down and fashioned into something new. Despite this, many ancient gold artefacts have survived – often in grave goods, like those at Varna – and due to the durability of this precious metal, the objects are as stunning today as when they were first made. An example is the golden funeral mask of the Egyptian pharaoh, Tutankhamun. The solid gold mask, weighing 10 kg and inlaid with turquoise, lapis lazuli, carnelian and coloured glass, retains its lustre after 3000 years.

FACTS

GOLD IS SO DENSE THAT 0.05 M³ WEIGHS 1 TONNE.
A piece of gold is six to seven times heavier than the matrix rock in which it is found.

A RARE
AMERICAN GOLD COIN
with a face value of $20 was sold for $7.59 million in 2002.

THE JEWELLERY INDUSTRY USES
2000 TONNES OF GOLD
each year; dentistry uses 87 tonnes.

FACTS

A VERSATILE METAL

FROM SACRED OBJECTS TO FOOD DECORATION, FROM ARCHITECTURAL ORNAMENT TO FILLINGS FOR TEETH, THE USES TO WHICH GOLD HAS BEEN PUT ARE EXTREMELY VARIED. It can be beaten into thin sheets of gold leaf and used to cover a variety of surfaces to give the appearance of solid gold. As gold is non-toxic and tasteless, it has been used as food decoration and in medicines since ancient times. And as it can reflect infrared and ultraviolet light, it is incorporated into glass for use in buildings and in spacecraft.

Creating the look of solid gold

The ancient Egyptians were the first people to master the art of hammering gold into thin sheets. The earliest surviving examples of gilding, dating from around 3000 BC, are silver statues wrapped in gold foil. Since then, it has been applied to a range of

GOLDEN GODS Craftspeople in Thailand apply gold leaf to statues of the Buddha and other sacred objects.

surfaces, including metal, wood and plaster, to produce sacred and valuable objects, including statues, paintings, picture frames and altarpieces. Thai Buddhists attach small squares of gold leaf to statues of the Buddha to gain merit. In the Mahamuni temple in Myanmar (formerly Burma), the country's oldest gold buddha has had so much gold leaf attached to it by worshippers over the centuries that it has become barely recognisable. Gold leaf has also been used the world over on furniture and architectural mouldings in prestigious buildings. Perhaps the most spectacular examples of gold leaf have been for large expanses of walls and ceilings, from the three-storey Golden Pavilion in Kyoto, which is covered in gold leaf inside and out, to the Spanish Baroque churches of colonial South America, and Les Invalides in Paris housing the tomb of Napoleon, the dome of which is covered with gold leaf inside and out.

The traditional process for producing gold leaf is called goldbeating. The goldbeater takes a small ingot of gold and rolls it into a long ribbon 0.025 mm thick. He cuts the ribbon into 3 cm squares, places them between sheets of heavy paper and wraps them in leather. He hammers the leather bundle until the squares measure 10 cm on each side, then cuts each square into four, repacks them in heavy paper and leather and beats them again. The process is repeated several times until the gold leaf is just 0.18 microns thick – so thin that it cannot be handled with the fingers. Instead, it is picked up and positioned using a wide brush

WALLS OF GOLD The interior of the 17th-century church of La Compania in Quito, Ecuador, is covered in gold-leaf ornamentation.

known as a gilder's tip. Much modern gold leaf is produced in rolling mills, and is so thin that it is almost transparent.

Various methods of fixing gold leaf in place have been used. In Europe, medieval gilders began using an adhesive made from egg whites to apply the foil. Water gilding uses a glue of water and methylated spirits, while oil gilding uses an oil-based glue and is used for gilding the exteriors of buildings. Cheaper substitutes are available (such as 'Dutch metal', an alloy of zinc and copper), but gold leaf continues to be used in gilding because it gives a superior finish that does not tarnish with age.

Unexpected uses of gold

In recent years, gold leaf has found some unusual applications. In May 2007, a Japanese firm began offering a $300 gold-leaf facial. The idea is that laying thin sheets of gold on the face helps with rejuvenation, firming the skin and reducing wrinkles. Gold leaf has also been used as a coating for gourmet chocolates. Although not particularly tasty, gold is perfectly non-toxic, and the gold foil keeps the chocolates fresh.

Medicinal uses

Gold is unreactive within the body, or 'biocompatible'. Unlike nickel, for instance, which can cause an allergic reaction when worn next to the skin, pure gold is hypoallergenic, which makes it suitable for many medical applications. Drugs containing gold compounds, such as Myocrisin and Auranofin, have been used to treat inflammatory illnesses, such as arthritis, and gold may have potential against HIV and cancer. It is also resistant to bacteria, which makes it useful for coating implants that may be at risk of infection, such as those designed for the inner ear.

Gold fillings are familiar in dentistry, but they are usually alloys of gold with other unreactive metals, such as platinum, palladium and silver. Pure gold would be too soft, so the other metals are added to give the alloy strength. Gold is used to make fillings, crowns and bridges, the content varying with the application. A gold crown may be about 70 per cent gold.

Reflective glass

In addition to its many other qualities, gold is used in glass to reflect heat but not light. A very thin coating – just 1 g of gold is needed to cover 10 m² of glass – can reflect 98 per cent of infrared light while letting visible light through. Windows using this type of glass reflect heat in summer while letting light through. They also retain heat inside the building in winter, providing an effective means of energy conservation. Gold glass has been known to cut a building's heating and air-conditioning costs by 40 per cent. Because of its ability to reflect intense heat, gold coatings are also used for the visors of spacesuits and the windscreens of high-altitude aircraft.

LUCKY STRIKES

ON FEBRUARY 5, 1869, AUSTRALIAN GOLD PROSPECTOR JOHN DEASON WAS WORKING THE GROUND IN MOLIAGUL, VICTORIA, WHEN HE CHANCED UPON THE FIND OF A LIFETIME. He had hit on an enormous gold nugget weighing some 71 kg. Known as the 'Welcome Stranger', it remains the largest gold nugget ever recorded. Deason and his partner cashed it in for £9000. At today's price of $650 per troy ounce, the nugget would be worth around $1.5 million.

Many of the biggest early gold finds were, like Deason's, made by accident. Once news got out about a find, or strike, adventurers would flock to the area hoping to make their fortunes. In 1848, carpenter James Marshall was building a sawmill at Coloma on a tributary of the American River in California. While deepening the millstream he spotted something yellow in the ground. The object was about the size of

At least 13 million people in over 30 developing countries engage in small-scale gold mining, with some 80–100 million people depending on it for their livelihood.

INDIVIDUAL ENTERPRISE Wild-cat miners pan for gold in the Amazonian rainforest. They move from site to site as areas become panned out.

GOLD DEPOSIT Gold flakes panned from the Juma River in Brazil. While other sediments float to the water's surface, gold sinks to the bottom of the pan.

a pea, but it was pure gold, and other people found pieces in the area, too. Word spread and before long thousands of prospectors descended upon the Sierra Nevada region of California and the largest gold rush in history began.

'Gold is where you find it'

Even after the excessive activity of the 19th-century gold rushes, there is still gold to be discovered. Prospectors have a saying: 'Gold is where you find it.' They know that all the theory means nothing unless you use your eyes, so even if you are in an area where gold has been found, you need to know where to look.

'Two things are essential,' says British gold-panner Alf Henderson, who has prospected all over the world. 'You require moving water, and the water must have come through an area where there has been volcanic activity or heat associated with formations in the Earth's crust so that minerals have been deposited. We're talking about granite and slate. The gold was removed from the rocks by water. When the water slowed down it deposited the gold in deep cracks, fissures in rocks, outcrops and boulders.' So the key is to look for bends in a river where the flow of water is slowed and it may have set down the gold; or to work out where an ancient river might once have meandered. 'You are looking

AMAZON GOLD Independent miners and small companies have cleared areas of the rainforest in Brazil in pursuit of surface deposits of gold.

for places where you can get down to the bedrock,' says Alf. 'Gold is heavy; it wants to be at the lowest possible point it can get. If you can get down to bedrock, the gold can go no further.' Alf's biggest find was 16.5 oz in just eight days. Its hiding place couldn't have been more apt: a region called Treasure Hill at the top of Last Chance Creek, in the Klondike, Yukon, Canada. 'I was fiddling about and I found a little vein of gold ... Some movement had occurred and uplifted this line of what was once an ancient riverbed. It was a 6 in seam of gravel and you could work it out with a stick.'

Wild-cat gold miners

For Alf Henderson, gold panning is an absorbing hobby, but many people earn a living from panning for gold. According to the World Bank's Community and Small-Scale Mining Initiative, at least 13 million people worldwide in over 30 developing countries engage in small-scale mining, with some 80–100 million people depending on it for their livelihood. Though indigenous peoples have mined and panned for gold in their localities for centuries and see it as a cultural right, there are problems associated with this type of mining. Mercury amalgamation is often used to extract the gold, a process that can be harmful to the environment. Large companies follow strict guidelines and laws governing how chemicals and waste from goldmines are treated, but small-scale mines and lone miners slip through the net. The Global Mercury Project (GMP) was set up in 2002 to try to limit the mercury contamination of international waters from small-scale goldmining. Six countries are participating in the project: Brazil, Laos, Indonesia, Sudan, Tanzania and Zimbabwe. The GMP aims to introduce cleaner technologies, train miners to use them and develop enforceable regulations that will minimise mercury pollution.

INDUSTRIAL GOLD

GOLD CAN BE FOUND IN TINY AMOUNTS ALL OVER THE WORLD. On average, there is 5 mg of gold for every tonne of the Earth's crust. This amount is not worth recovering – you would need some 2000 tonnes of rock to make a wedding ring. But in a few places gold is present in deposits large enough to make extraction worthwhile. For a gold mine to be viable, the ore needs to contain 2–10 g of gold per tonne of rock, depending on the depth of the mine and the method of extraction.

Gold ore can be found in rocks of all ages, often around modern and ancient tectonic plate boundaries. The primary deposits occur in 'greenstones', ancient basaltic lavas that were laid down during the Earth's early history. Over millions of years the gold has been removed from this rock and carried in solution in extremely hot water

SUPERPIT Measuring nearly 4 km long and 1.5 km wide, the Kalgoorlie open-cut pit is Australia's largest gold mine. It is 500 m deep, and trucks take 20 minutes to haul ore to the surface.

AT THE ROCK FACE South Africa's gold mines are the deepest in the world. Conditions are cramped, and in some the rock is too hot to touch.

(hydrothermal solutions) through fractures and fissures in other types of rock, eventually being deposited as veins, or lodes, as the solution cooled. Where gold has been washed out of the source rock and carried to another location, such as a stream bed, it collects in placer deposits. These may be recent or, like the Witwatersrand basin of South Africa, they may be an ancient deposit that has since been buried.

In geologically active regions of the world, such as Yellowstone National Park in the USA, and parts of the Andes, geothermal gold is still being deposited. Geologists study these modern-day sites for clues on where to look for ancient deposits. Placer deposits – which have triggered so many gold rushes around the world – are still forming.

Mining methods

There are two methods for mining gold. When a deposit is relatively shallow, an open-pit mine is economical and the gold need only be concentrated to 2 g per tonne of rock. The rock is blasted away with explosives and taken to a mill to be processed. Deeper deposits are extracted from underground workings via deep shafts. This is a more expensive process, so the deposit has to be more concentrated in order for extraction to be viable.

The cheapest mechanised method for recovering gold is the gravity separation process. This is always used when gold is recovered from placer deposits in gravels because gold usually occurs there in its free state. Some of the gold from hardrock deposits can be recovered in this way after the matrix rock has been crushed. The rest has to be extracted using chemicals.

Working in a gold mine

Some of the deepest mines in the world are gold mines, reaching depths of 4 km. At such depths, the temperature can be above 40°C, which may cause miners to pass out from heat exhaustion. Air-conditioning units are installed in some of the deeper mines, and keeping the temperature in a mine at a just tolerable 32°C can be one of the highest costs incurred in an underground mining project. Even then, humidity can approach 100 per cent.

Geologist Jim Williams, chief executive of Arian Silver, has been down several mines in South Africa and other parts of the world, the deepest of which was about 2.5 km. He says that stepping into a deep mine is 'like stepping into a sauna'. But the extreme heat is not the only hazard of working deep in the crust. At such depths, rock bursts – shards of rock exploding out from the walls of the mine like flying shrapnel – are common. 'As soon as you put a hole in a piece of rock you have pressures acting against you, and some of the pressures in deep mines are phenomenal,' says Jim. 'Chips spit off and if they hit you they hurt you – sometimes fatally. Rock bursts can be quite small and it's a bit like being fired at with an airgun pellet.' Some rock bursts are much larger and may even cause part of a mine to collapse, although there is usually some warning. If a mine is too costly to shore up and too dangerous to work, it has to be abandoned.

FACTS

THE OCEANS CONTAIN ABOUT 0.02 MG OF GOLD per litre of seawater, which amounts to about 20 million tonnes in total, but extraction costs would be too high for this to be worthwhile.

ONLY 41 000 TONNES of gold are estimated to be left in the Earth for extraction.

NEARLY 40 PER CENT of all the gold ever mined has come from South Africa.

FACTS

SMELTING GOLD

THOUGH GOLD CAN BE FOUND IN ITS NATIVE, METALLIC STATE, MOST GOLD THAT IS MINED HAS TO BE EXTRACTED FROM ITS ORE. As gold is one of the least soluble substances known, its extraction requires a series of complex processes before the metal can be smelted and purified. The earliest methods of extraction involved crushing up the ore by hand and treating it with mercury to make an amalgam. The amalgam was then boiled to drive off the mercury as a vapour and leave the gold behind.

Mercury vapour is highly toxic, both in the environment and for the health of those working in the industry, and this method is no longer used in modern industrial gold-processing plants. Gold also dissolves in sodium cyanide solution, and modern plants use this chemical instead. Of course, cyanide is also poisonous and it is no surprise that gold extraction plants have to follow strict laws concerning how they protect their workers – they always have a cyanide antidote on site – and how they dispose of any waste.

The gold is mixed with fluxes that draw out impurities and heated for several hours in a furnace that reaches 1200°C. This is repeated several times, then the gold is poured into moulds to produce ingots.

Extraction and recovery

The first stage of extraction involves crushing the ore to produce fist-sized pieces, and grinding these in large rotating drums containing steel balls that bounce around and crush the rock into fine particles. The second stage consists of using chemicals to separate out the gold. The particles are mixed with water to make a slurry, and sodium cyanide solution is added to separate the gold from the ore. Grains of carbon are mixed into the solution and the dissolved gold collects as a thin film on the grains. Carbon is used because it has a very large surface area – 1 g of carbon has the same surface area as a tennis court – and absorbs most of the gold from the sludge.

The gold-laden carbon is pumped through a circuit where the gold is washed off, and the gold is precipitated out of this solution by electrowinning, which involves placing the solution in an electrolytic cell containing steel wool. When an electric current is passed through the solution, the gold is deposited on the steel wool, which is then rinsed to produce a gold-bearing sludge.

After that, the sludge is mixed with fluxes that draw out impurities and heated for several hours in a furnace that reaches a temperature of 1200°C. The molten gold is poured into crucibles and shipped to plants that continue the refining process. When the gold has reached the required level of purity, it is poured in moulds to produce gold bars, or ingots. These are stamped with the manufacturer's name, the precise weight

GOLD BARS At a refinery for precious metals in Los Angeles, workers pour purified gold into moulds to produce ingots.

LIQUID GOLD At a Johannesburg gold mine molten gold cascades down a series of crucibles to produce bars that will be sent for further refining.

GOLD LEGENDS

Many legends have sprung up about gold, most of them concerning the pursuit of some hidden treasure. One of the oldest is the Greek myth of King Midas. When the god Dionysus offered him a single wish, King Midas asked for everything he touched to turn to gold. The wish was granted and he was initially happy, but the tale is a warning against the shallow pleasures of material things. King Midas found that he could not eat because his food turned to gold, and when he touched his daughter, she, too, turned to gold.

An old German folk story called the *Nibelungenlied*, tells of a race of dwarves who steal gold from the rhinemaidens. One of the dwarves makes a golden ring that grants the power to rule the world. The story inspired Richard Wagner's 'Ring cycle' of operas.

In the 16th century, Spanish adventurers headed for South America in search of 'El Dorado' (the golden man), a wealthy native king. They believed that he had gold dust sprinkled on his skin each day and washed it off in a lake, which some people believed was Lake Guatavita in Colombia. The story may have arisen because gold was found in such abundance in South America and had long been mined by native people.

STOCKPILED GOLD

GOLD RESERVE Gold bars worth US $5.2 million go on display in Poland's National Bank.

Sited five floors below street level on Manhattan bedrock – the only foundation strong enough to take the weight – the Federal Reserve Bank of New York's vaults hold about 7000 tonnes of gold, the largest stockpile in the world.

BECAUSE OF GOLD'S INTRINSIC VALUE, IT HAS OFTEN BEEN USED FOR CURRENCY. By making a coin from a fixed weight of gold, that coin had a set value. If it had an official stamp, traders could trust the coin and did not have to weigh every one. The first coins were made of electrum, a natural mixture of gold and 20 per cent silver. The coins, stamped with various designs, date from 700 BC and were used in Lydia, part of modern-day Turkey. The Romans used bronze coins as currency at first, introducing silver and gold coins in about 150 BC. The *aureus denarius*, or gold penny, was in use until AD 250.

Over time, countries switched to using alloys of gold and less valuable metals, such as copper and nickel, for currency, and then to paper money. Yet gold has always retained a high value. In the early 18th century, British bankers began the practice of defining the value of their currency (paper notes and metal coins) in terms of gold, by setting a price for 1 troy ounce. This became known as the 'gold standard' and was adopted by many other countries. Gold kept for this purpose was called bullion. It made trading easier and led to many countries amassing huge stockpiles.

In 1968, the gold standard was abolished, and licensed dealers have been able to buy and sell gold on the international open market. Like any commodity, its value can go up and down. The fluctuating price of gold has led some countries, including Great Britain, to sell off some of their gold bullion. When a country sells off a substantial part of its reserve, the gold market becomes flooded and the price of gold inevitably falls. Because of this effect, countries sign international agreements that limit the amount of gold they can sell at any one time.

Stacks of gold

Today, the greatest gold reserves are in the USA, Germany and France. The largest single stockpile of gold is in the Federal Reserve Bank of New York. Sited five floors below street level on Manhattan bedrock – the only foundation strong enough to take the weight – the bank's vaults hold about 7000 tonnes of gold bars. Stacked in anonymous compartments, the alluring metal is seen only by the CCTV monitors. Charged with guarding the gold reserves of about 60 clients – countries, central banks and

GOLD RESERVES BY COUNTRY	
COUNTRY	TONNES
USA	8133.5
Germany	3422.5
France	2709.6
Italy	2451.8
Switzerland	1290.1
Japan	765.2
Netherlands	640.9
China	600.0
Taiwan	423.3
Spain	416.8

international organisations – the Federal Reserve Bank takes security very seriously. There are no doors into the vault: entry is via a narrow passageway cut into a 90 tonne steel cylinder that rotates inside a steel-and-concrete frame. The vault is opened and closed by rotating the cylinder. Combination and time locks secure the vault, with no single employee knowing the whole combination. Of the 7000 tonnes of gold stored there, only 400 tonnes belong to the US government. Most of the rest of the USA's reserve – 4583 tonnes of it – is held at Fort Knox, Kentucky.

Bricks, boats and doughnuts

Gold bullion is normally stored in the form of metal bars, or ingots. Most gold in international banks is held as London Good Delivery Bars, each weighing 400 troy ounces (12.5 kg) and with a minimum purity of 99.5 per cent. According to the World Gold Council, there are only 55 manufacturers whose 400 oz bars are accepted internationally as London Good Delivery. But gold bars come in many shapes and sizes. The kilobar, which is brick shaped or flat and weighs 1 kg, is the most widely traded small gold bar. The tael gold bar is traded in Chinese-speaking countries, such as Hong Kong and Taiwan. One tael weighs 37.4 g, and the bars are cast as biscuits, boats or doughnuts. The most popular is the biscuit-shaped 5 tael bar (187 g). The doughnut shape is used for small amounts, such as 1 or 2 tael; the hole in the middle allows the bars to be stacked on a rod or held together with cord.

MEASURING PURITY A bank worker in Zurich, Switzerland, uses an electronic device to check the purity of a holding of gold ingots.

PRECIOUS METALS

THERE ARE ONLY THREE METALS APART FROM GOLD THAT OCCUR NATURALLY IN THEIR METALLIC, OR NATIVE, STATE. These are copper, silver and platinum. These native metals share similar qualities. They all have great inherent beauty, they are malleable and ductile, making them easy to work, and they are less reactive than most other elements. Being readily available in nature, they all have a long history of use. All except copper are rare and have been used for currency. All have been used for making objects of beauty, such as jewellery, and a whole range of practical and ornamental domestic items. Meanwhile, modern science continues to find new uses for these versatile, naturally occuring metals in a range of different products. They have been used in cancer drugs, superconductors, biomedical electrodes and catalytic converters for motor vehicles.

DIGGING DEEP One of the largest open-cast copper mines is in Brigham Canyon, Utah. When copper is exposed to the environment, oxidation can produce green salts (above).

COPPER

THE REDDISH COLOUR OF COPPER IS UNMISTAKEABLE. IT IS MUCH MORE ABUNDANT THAN GOLD, SILVER AND PLATINUM, AND WAS THE FIRST METAL TO BE WIDELY USED FOR TOOLS, WEAPONS AND COOKING IMPLEMENTS. Another characteristic of copper is that, unlike most metals, it can be used in its pure state. The earliest recorded use of copper was in northern Iraq in 8500 BC. It was being used in Egypt by 7000 BC. The Romans mined copper in Cyprus, calling it cyprium, meaning 'the metal from Cyprus'. It was later shortened to cuprum, hence its chemical symbol Cu. Today the greatest reserves are in Chile, which produces a third of the world's supply. Copper is mined on a gigantic scale in open-cast and underground mines. The largest open-pit mine in the world is a copper mine near Chuquicamata in the Antofagasta region of northern Chile. El Teniente, another Chilean copper mine, is the world's largest underground mine.

Copper is soft, ductile and a good electrical and thermal conductor. You need only look around your house to see how much we depend on copper. Formed into sheets, plates, rods, bars, pipes and wire – this versatile metal has a multitude of uses. Most watertanks are copper, as are the pipes carrying water around the house. All the wiring in your house is made of copper, and it is an important component of electrical equipment, such as telephones, televisions, computers and anything containing an electromagnet. Because of its excellent heat conductivity, copper has traditionally been used to make saucepans and other cooking utensils.

Copper and its compounds and alloys have bactericidal and fungicidal properties. Copper sulphate is an effective fungicide, and even the earliest medical texts refer to the use of copper compounds to disinfect wounds and promote healing. Copper pipes help to reduce the number of bacteria present in water. And old-fashioned copper and brass doorknobs are more hygienic than modern substitutes since they naturally disinfect themselves within a few hours.

In industry, copper is found in valves, heat exchangers and the coils used in electromagnetic generators. It is an important component in the electrical systems of motor vehicles and spacecraft. One of the most recent uses for copper is in superconducting ceramics, which contain copper compounds.

RENEWABLE ENERGY In India, copper is being used in the manufacture of generators for wind turbines.

SILVER

FOR THE LAST WEEK IN NOVEMBER, THE QUIET MEXICAN HILLTOWN OF TAXCO BECOMES THE CENTRE OF THE WORLD FOR SILVERSMITHS AND ALL WHO LOVE THIS LUSTROUS METAL. Crowds of artisans bustle through the narrow, cobblestoned streets to take part in the Feria Nacional de La Plata – the annual silver fair – in the hope of winning a prize. Sunglasses are essential as the streets literally dazzle with fine silver sculptures, delicate filigreework, silverware and all types of jewellery glinting in the Mexican sun.

Situated about 125 km south-west of Mexico City, Taxco has a long connection with silver. It is the site of some of the oldest silver mine workings in the Americas. In the early 16th century, its wealth of silver attracted the attention of the Spanish conquistadors. After conquering the Aztecs in 1521, Hernán Cortés came to Taxco and promptly staked a claim. By the end of the century, the small town's fame had spread around the world. But as better deposits were found elsewhere, its silver mining declined. It was revived in 1716 when a rich vein of silver was found in the hills around Taxco. In the 1920s, a highway finally linked Taxco with Mexico City. The road became known as 'the silver road' as it allowed the easy transport and trade of the metal. More recently, a school of silversmithing has been established in Taxco to encourage the local people to create traditional designs. The community of craftsmen has steadily grown and today the town has hundreds of silver shops.

Mexico remains a world leader in silver production alongside Peru, China and Australia. This is due to a rich source of silver ore in the stretch of mountains that run along the western edge of the Pacific 'Ring of Fire'.

GEORG JENSEN JEWELLERY
The malleability of silver makes it a suitable meal for moulding into fine shapes, a quality exploited in this contemporary Georg Jensen necklace.

Geological activity has concentrated the silver ore here through the movement of hydrothermal fluids. Although other countries produce silver bullion and commemorative coins, Mexico is the only country that still uses silver in its currency, though not in its pure state. According to the Silver Institute, in 2005 more than half the silver produced around the world was used in industrial applications, while about a quarter went into the jewellery and silverware markets.

Another important market for silver is the photographic industry. The photographic process relies on silver halide crystals layered on unexposed film, which change when exposed to light. Though the digital revolution has had a huge impact on the photographic industry, silver-based photography still produces images of superior quality. Silver-based film is used in non-destructive testing of metallic components since silver halide X-ray film is best at showing up any flaws.

A key industrial application of silver is as a catalyst (a chemical that enhances a reaction while not being changed by the reaction itself). The billion-pound plastics industry relies on silver in the production of two vital components: ethylene oxide, the building block for flexible plastics, including polyester textiles; and formaldehyde, an important industrial chemical and the building block for rigid plastics. Silver's superior electrical conductivity, its low contact resistance, its resistance to corrosion and its cost-effectiveness mean that it

SUPERIOR TABLEWARE
This soup tureen is from an 18th-century French dinner service. Silver has always been popular for tableware because it is easily shaped and embossed, and it can be polished to a high shine.

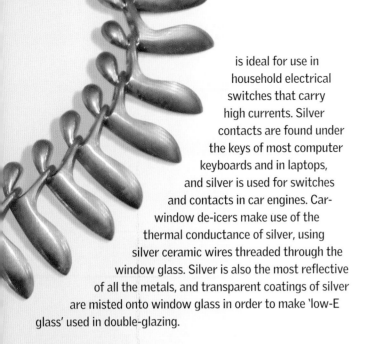

is ideal for use in household electrical switches that carry high currents. Silver contacts are found under the keys of most computer keyboards and in laptops, and silver is used for switches and contacts in car engines. Car-window de-icers make use of the thermal conductance of silver, using silver ceramic wires threaded through the window glass. Silver is also the most reflective of all the metals, and transparent coatings of silver are misted onto window glass in order to make 'low-E glass' used in double-glazing.

Sterling silver

Pure silver is too soft for most purposes and it is normally alloyed with copper to improve its hardness and strength. Sterling silver – 92.5 per cent silver and 7.5 per cent copper – has been a standard for jewellery and silverware since the Middle Ages. The name sterling has been in use since the 13th century, when the English imported silver coins from eastern Europe, calling them 'easterlings' and stamping them with a star. The purity, or 'fineness', of silver is measured in thousandths, like gold, so sterling silver is 925 fine.

Hallmarks for sterling silver vary from country to country. British sterling silver normally has the stamp of a lion, plus a letter to indicate the year in which the item was made. Another symbol indicates where the piece was manufactured, such as a crown for Sheffield (a city renowned for its high-quality silverware). Some countries, such as the USA, never adopted a standard mark for sterling silver and most hallmarks simply describe who made the item, such as 'T & Co' for jewellers Tiffany & Co.

Silver tableware became fashionable in the 18th century. Due to its malleability, silver was worked into a variety of shapes to produce terrines, cutlery, coffee pots, ladles, gravy dishes and sugar bowls. These were decorated and embossed with a range of motifs that reflected architectural and interior design styles of the day. A full dinner service could comprise more than 100 pieces. Nobility often had the silverware embellished with the family's coat of arms.

For those who couldn't afford sterling silver, there was silver plate. The process for laying a fine coating of silver over copper was developed in the 18th century. A layer of silver is fused to both sides of a sheet of base metal – copper, brass, steel or 'nickel silver' (an alloy of nickel, copper and zinc) – and the sandwich is worked into the finished object. In 1840, the electroplating process was developed: an electric current is used to deposit a fine layer of sterling silver onto a base metal. The electroplating industry began in Birmingham, England, and soon spread around the world. Electroplated items look like solid silver, but can be identified by the mark 'EPNS' (electroplated nickel silver).

PLATINUM

TODAY, PLATINUM IS MORE VALUABLE THAN GOLD AND IS USED FOR THE FINEST AND MOST FASHIONABLE JEWELLERY. But when it was discovered in the early 16th century, after the Spanish had colonised South America, it was regarded as an unwanted impurity in silver and gold. The metal was difficult to extract and refine and little was done with it until the early 19th century. Today, the largest platinum deposit is found in the Bushveld Igneous Complex of South Africa. Notable deposits are also found in Russia. South Africa and Russia together supply 90 per cent of the world's platinum.

Platinum's main use is as a catalyst in a wide range of chemical processes and in petroleum refining, including as an emission-control catalyst in motor vehicles. A combination of platinum, rhodium and palladium are dispersed onto a ceramic or metal honeycomb structure, through which the exhaust fumes pass. As the fumes travel through the chamber, 90 per cent of carbon dioxide, hydrocarbons and nitrogen oxides are removed.

RARE NUGGET The grey-white colour of platinum has become synonymous with prestige and exclusivity.

Like gold, platinum is inert and is used for biomedical devices. Platinum coils are used for treating aneurysms, while platinum alloys tend to be used as biomedical electrodes – as in the platinum-iridium wires of pacemaker leads. Platinum is also used in the anti-cancer drugs Carboplatin and Cisplatin.

The metal's high status is exemplified in a piece of contemporary art. In 2007, the artist Damien Hirst chose platinum for a life-size replica of a human skull. The skull is encrusted with 8600 small diamonds and has a large pear-shaped diamond in the forehead. Called 'For the Love of God', it went on sale for £50 million. The materials alone are worth at least £15 million.

DIAMONDS

A DIAMOND, AS THE SAYING GOES, IS FOR EVER, AND AS A LASTING SYMBOL OF LOVE IT IS UNSURPASSED. The word 'diamond' comes from the Greek *adamas*, meaning 'unconquerable', a highly appropriate description of the hardest material known to man.

Diamonds are made from the same substance as graphite. Both are made from carbon, but it is the way the carbon atoms are held that determines whether you have pencil lead or a glittering stone. In graphite the carbon atoms are held in long sheets, which can slip over each other, while in diamonds the atoms are held in a rigid lattice, giving it its supreme strength.

Every natural diamond is a time traveller as each crystal formed billions of years ago in the depths of the Earth. At 200 km below the surface, the intense pressure and temperature squeezed the carbon atoms together so that they formed the regular and exceedingly strong crystal structure. Volcanic activity has brought the diamonds up towards the surface in 'pipes' of rock that form as magma is cooled. Over hundreds of millions of years the volcanic rock weathers away, exposing some of the diamonds. Some may wash down into rivers or beaches, while others remain in the pipes.

DIAMOND CRATER Opened in 1957, the Mir diamond mine in East Siberia spirals 600 m into the ground. While in operation, the mine, which finally closed in 2004, yielded around two million carats per year.

Alluvial deposits

Before the mid-19th century, diamonds were found only in sources where they had washed out of the rock. These are known as alluvial deposits and India was the major source. Some of the world's finest diamonds have come from the Golconda diamond fields, near Hyderabad. In the 1660s, the celebrated French jeweller and traveller Jean-Baptiste Tavernier visited Golconda and described how thousands of men dug pits 3–4 m deep, while the women and children carried the conglomerate away in baskets to be washed and sorted. In 1725, diamonds were discovered in Brazil, and in the years that followed the Brazilian alluvial fields began to supersede those of India. One of the last great diamonds to be mined at Golconda was the Nizam diamond, a massive 440-carat stone found in 1835.

Since diamonds are so hard, they can travel great distances from where they were washed out of the rock and remain perfectly intact. Only diamonds with flaws or cracks will be destroyed, so that the finest gem-quality stones are naturally sorted. Such a process has led to an abundance of fine diamonds along the Namibian coast in southern Africa, which today are mined from the beach gravels in large open pits. The yield is around 5 carats of diamonds for every 150 tonnes of gravel lifted, an extraction that remains economical as most of the diamonds are the highest quality gemstones.

The largest diamond retrieved from an alluvial source is the Star of Sierra Leone, discovered, appropriately, on Valentine's Day in 1972. Workers at the rich Kono diamond fields in Sierra Leone, in West Africa, gasped in amazement as the huge diamond moved along the picking table amongst the rubble and other smaller fragments. The stone was the size of a hen's egg and weighed 969 carats.

Diamond mines

Modern-day diamond mining began in 1866 with the chance discovery of an alluvial diamond in the gravels of the Orange River, in South Africa. Soon the country became a magnet for diamond hunters. A number of diamonds were found on land that had formerly belonged to two brothers, Johannes Nicholas and Diederik Arnoldus de Beer, whose name survives in that of the world's biggest diamond corporation, De Beers.

Geologists discovered that diamonds found in South Africa's Kimberley region were coming from a then unknown source rock – the pipes of ancient volcanoes. The rock was named kimberlite, and since its discovery more pipes containing diamonds have been located all over the world. Today, the top five diamond-producing countries are Botswana, Russia, Australia, the Democratic Republic of Congo and Canada. Russia alone accounts for about 21 per cent of global diamond production, most of which is mined in Siberia, just below the Arctic Circle. Currently, the world market for uncut diamonds is worth more than £5 billion annually.

Mining the enormous carrot-shaped kimberlite pipes, which may be up to 1.5 km across and reach depths of 3 km, takes place on a massive scale. Kimberlite contains about 25 carats of diamond per 100 tonnes of mined rock. Of this just 5 carats is likely to be gem quality. Diamonds that are not good enough to be cut into gems can be adapted for use in lathes, drills and saws, or as an abrasive.

Extracting diamonds from the matrix rock relies on the unique properties of diamond. First, the rock or gravel is crushed, and heavy minerals including diamonds are removed. This matter may then be loaded onto a greasebelt and a stream of water used to wash away everything apart from the diamonds, which stick to the grease. Another method uses the fact that diamonds fluoresce when an X-ray beam is shone at them. The fluorescing diamonds are identified by an instrument that puffs a blast of air to move them off the conveyer belt.

MIXED GEMS A scatter of diamond crystals shows the variations in colour from transparent through to yellow, brown and pink hues.

NATURAL STATE A rough diamond embedded in kimberlite. The rock occurs in the Earth's crust in vertical structures known as kimberlite pipes, the main source of diamonds mined today.

Legendary gems

Perhaps the most famous diamond of them all is the Koh-i-Noor. The name means 'Mountain of Light' and it has a long and fascinating history. Now part of the British Crown Jewels, the diamond was found in India, at Golconda, according to some sources more than 5000 years ago. It passed into the hands of a succession of rulers, including the Mughal ruler Shah Jahan who built the Taj Mahal and had the stone placed into his ornate Peacock Throne. In 1849, the stone was presented to Queen Victoria and it was re-cut to produce the current 108.93-carat jewel set in the crown worn by Queen Elizabeth at the coronation of her husband, George VI. The Koh-i-Noor diamond is said to bring misfortune or death to any male who wears or owns it, but good fortune to female owners.

Another famous diamond with a long and colourful past is the Black Orlov. The story goes that the stone was removed from a Hindu shrine near Pondicherry in India. A monk prised the rough 195-carat stone out of the eye of an idol of Brahma and the stone has been cursed ever since. In 1932, J.W. Paris, the diamond dealer who imported the diamond to the USA, is said to have jumped to his death from the top of a New York building. Two similar deaths followed by people who had owned the stone. The first was Princess Leonila Galitsine-Bariatinsky, who leapt to her death in November 1947. Just a month later a Russian princess, Nadia Vyegin-Orlov, who had owned the gem in the late 18th century, is said to have also committed suicide by jumping to her death. Whatever its malign influence, there is no denying the rare gem's beauty. A deep gun-metal colour, the 67.50-carat cushion-cut stone is set within a brooch of 108 white diamonds and suspended from a 124-diamond necklace.

Another so-called cursed diamond is the blue Hope diamond, named after Henry Philip Hope, an avid collector of gems, who owned the diamond in the 1830s. Renowned for its rare, deep sapphire blue colour, the 45.52-carat Hope diamond is also reputed to bring misfortune and death to its owners.

Diamonds in the sky

In 2004, astronomers discovered the ultimate diamond – the size of our Moon and located at the heart of a dead star. The ten billion trillion trillion-carat gem is located in the Centaurus constellation some 50 light years away. The cosmic diamond is actually a crystallised white dwarf, the hot core that remains when a star runs out of fuel. Astronomers at the Harvard-Smithsonian Center for Astrophysics, who discovered the diamond, say that the white dwarf, officially known as BPM 37093, but nicknamed Lucy, is not only twinkling, but also rings like an enormous gong as it continually pulsates. By measuring these pulsations, the astronomers were able to conclude that the carbon interior of this white dwarf has solidifed to form the galaxy's largest diamond. Astronomers predict that in five billion years' time our Sun, too, will become a white dwarf when it dies. Some two billion years after that its core will also crystallise, leaving a diamond at the centre of our solar system – perhaps the only sign that we were ever here.

The Four Cs

The criteria used to assess the value of a particular diamond are: carat, clarity, colour and cut – known as the 'Four Cs'. The carat describes how much a diamond weighs, where 5 carats are equal to 1 g. The carat is further divided into 100 'points', allowing gems to be weighed – and hence valued – very precisely. Generally, the larger the stone, the more valuable it is. Total carat weight (t.c.w.) describes the total mass of diamonds in a piece of jewellery, such as earrings, bracelets and necklaces.

DEEP BLUE Traces of boron give the famous Hope diamond its brilliant blue coloration. The 45.52-carat beauty is set in a pendant of 16 white diamonds. Some say that the doomed French queen Marie Antoinette wore the diamond.

A diamond's clarity rating depends on the number of defects – or inclusions – visible at 10x magnification. Inclusions, such as crystals of foreign materials or structural flaws, may not affect how much the diamond sparkles, but they lower its price. Only around 20 per cent of all diamonds mined have a clarity rating considered high enough for gemstone quality. Of that 20 per cent, a significant portion contains one or more visible inclusions. The top grade is flawless (FL), the lowest, with inclusions visible to the naked eye, is imperfect (I).

The colour of any gemstone depends on how light travels through it and this depends on the crystal structure of the gemstone and any impurities it contains. The purest diamond contains only carbon atoms in a uniform lattice and it is completely colourless. A colour scale grades 'colourless' or 'white' diamonds ranging from D to Z, with D being 'colourless' and Z having a bright yellow coloration. Since most diamonds contain some impurities, giving them a yellowish tinge, D-grade diamonds, especially large stones, are very rare.

Natural colours

Sometimes diamonds are naturally coloured and, depending on the intensity and uniformity of the colour, can be extremely valuable. The most common colours are yellow, orange and brown. Deep green and deep blue are less common, while red, violet and purple are the rarest shades. These 'fancy' colours result from either a deformation of the crystal lattice (the way the carbon atoms are held together) or the presence of impurities. The yellows, oranges and browns are produced by trapped nitrogen atoms, while tiny traces of trapped boron atoms are responsible for the stunning blue diamonds, such as the Hope diamond (above). A twisting of the diamond's crystal lattice gives rise to the rarest purple, pink and red 'fancy' colours. Black diamonds, like the famous Black Orlov, contain tiny inclusions of the minerals magnetite and haematite. Green diamonds can form after being subjected to millions of years of radiation. Often the radiation is from tiny alpha particles in the magma or kimberlite. Long exposure over geological time forms a green patch or a film on the surface of the diamond. Bombardment by stronger beta and gamma radiation may penetrate further, producing colour throughout the whole stone. The Dresden Green diamond is unique among coloured gems – an apple-green colour through and through.

CUTTING DIAMONDS

PRECISION CUTTING A diamond held ready for cutting around the midsection, also known as the stone's girdle, with a blade impregnated with diamond dust. A green marker helps the cutter to determine where to make the cuts.

Transforming a rough diamond into a gem is the art of the diamond cutter, who shapes and polishes the stone to reveal its sparkling qualities. After careful consideration of the stone's natural rough appearance and the location of imperfections, the cutter (or 'lapidary') decides on how to cut the stone to the most stunning effect, while keeping the stone as large as possible. The cutter marks in ink where cuts are to be made.

The diamond is then cut to create the gem's basic shape. Traditionally, large stones were preshaped before being sawed with a cleaver. A sharp hammer blow separated the stone into two carefully planned parts. Cleaving was a highly skilled operation as a mistake could shatter the stone completely.

Nowadays, cutting is usually done by sawing with a thin alloy blade impregnated with diamond dust. As the blade turns – at the speed of around 4000 revolutions a minute – it continues to be recharged by dust from the diamond. It can take anything from four to eight hours for the saw to cut through a 1-carat rough diamond. The sawn diamond is then crudely shaped into the round or other shape by rubbing it against another diamond on a high-speed lathe, in a process known as bruting or girdling.

Faceting

In order to exploit the stone's light and colour to the best advantage, facets (polished faces) are then produced by grinding the roughly shaped gem against a revolving disk in a process known as faceting. The most popular style of cut is the brilliant cut, a round stone with 58 facets. This was developed in 1919 by the Belgian mathematician and gem enthusiast Marcel Tolkowsky, who calculated the best proportions for cutting round brilliant diamonds.

Cuts that are not shaped to the specifications of Tolkowsky's round brilliant shape are known as 'fancy cuts' and include the emerald, baguette, heart-shaped, pear-shaped, kite and triangle. One fancy cut, the marquise, an elongated shape with pointed ends, was commissioned in the 18th century by the French king Louis XIV, who wanted a diamond to match the beguiling smile of his mistress, the Marquise de Pompadour. New and ever-more fanciful cuts continue to be developed, such as the square or rectangular princess cut.

Master cutter

In 1988, Gabi Tolkowsky, great nephew of Marcel Tolkowsky, was chosen to cut two record-breaking diamonds: the Centenary and the Golden Jubilee. Working with a team that included polishers, engineers, mathematicians and security guards in a secret workshop outside Johannesburg, South Africa, the project took three years. At 273.85 carats, the Centenary is the largest modern colourless flawless diamond in the world, while the Golden Jubilee – a whopping 545.67 carats – takes the crown as the largest faceted diamond ever.

The Golden Jubilee was presented to the King of Thailand to celebrate the 50th anniversary of his coronation. Prior to this it had simply been known as the Unnamed Brown. At first, no one believed that it had much potential and it was chosen by the diamond-cutting team for experimenting on and perfecting techniques that they would use on the Centenary. As cutting and polishing progressed, however, the gem's beauty was revealed: a fancy intense brown which has, as Gabi Tolkowsky describes it, 'the Sun in its heart'.

DIAMONDS CAN BE FOUND IN METEORITES THAT FALL TO EARTH.
Some of these interstellar travellers formed billions of years ago before our solar system existed.

IN 1969, RICHARD BURTON
lavished over $1 million dollars on a 69-carat pear-shaped diamond for his then wife Elizabeth Taylor.

MOST DIAMONDS
FOUND IN NATURE ARE between one and three billion years old.

GREAT STAR OF AFRICA

THE LARGEST ROUGH GEM-QUALITY DIAMOND

THE WORLD HAS EVER SEEN WAS THE CULLINAN DIAMOND FOUND IN 1905 at the Premier Diamond Mining Company near Johannesburg, South Africa. The raw 3106-carat diamond was presented by the Transvaal government to King Edward VII, and in 1908 it was dispatched to the Dutch firm I.J. Asscher for cutting.

The first nerve-racking attempt to cut the stone resulted in the cleaver knife breaking. At the second attempt the diamond was cleaved in two pieces. It was reported that the cutter, Joseph Asscher, fainted on the spot. Additional cleaving produced nine major stones, the largest of which was the mighty 530.20-carat, pear-shaped Great Star of Africa, also known as Cullinan I, which is now mounted in the Royal Sceptre of the British Crown Jewels (right). A brilliant cut gem normally has 58 facets, but because of its size, the Great Star of Africa was given 74 facets to reveal a jewel of outstanding beauty. It remained the world's largest cut diamond until it was surpassed by the 545.67-carat Golden Jubilee diamond, also found at the Premier Mine in 1985.

The second-largest gem from the Cullinan stone – known as Cullinan II or the Lesser Star of Africa – is the 317.40-carat cushion-shaped stone set in the Imperial State Crown, also part of the Crown Jewels housed in the Tower of London. Rumours abound of a second half of the Cullinan diamond. When it was found, experts became convinced that it was part of an even larger crystal that had broken off. The whereabouts of this missing twin remains a mystery.

GRADE: D-Flawless

DIMENSIONS: 58.9 x 45.4 mm

WEIGHT: 530.20 carats

SHAPE: Pear

FACETS: 74

VALUE: Priceless

DISCOVERED: At the Premier Diamond Mine near Johannesburg, South Africa, in 1905

VITAL STATISTICS

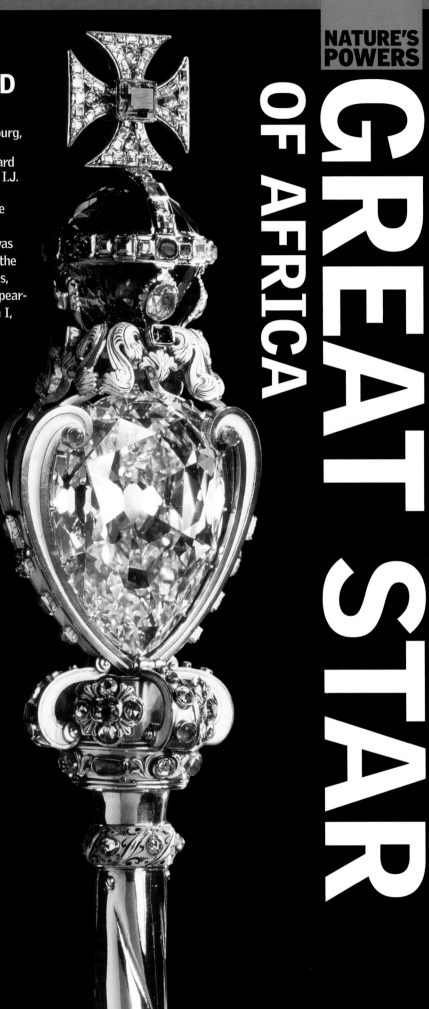

NATURE'S TREASURE CHEST

VALUED FOR THEIR BEAUTY, RARITY, COLOUR AND LUSTRE, gemstones are among the most highly prized of Earth's riches. Gem crystals form within the Earth as rocks and minerals shift and transform during the rock cycle (see page 38). Gems can be found in igneous, sedimentary and metamorphic rocks. Intrusive igneous rocks form below the Earth's surface and are created over millions of years as molten rock, or magma, slowly cools. Gem crystals form within the cooling magma. The slower the rock cools, the larger the crystals. One intrusive rock, pegmatite, yields many large gemstones, including aquamarine, topaz and tourmaline. Sometimes hot, mineral-laden liquids (hydrothermal fluids) find their way into cracks and cavities and later cool to form crystals such as amethyst and emerald. Extrusive igneous rocks, such as basalt, are strewn out violently by volcanic eruptions. The molten rock flows over the Earth's surface as lava which cools quickly. Gems that form in this lava include ruby, sapphire, moonstone and peridot. Sedimentary rocks, formed from compressed layers of sediment, contain turquoise, malachite, agate and opal. Metamorphic rocks – which form when existing rocks are subjected to extreme pressure and heat – can produce gems such as ruby, aquamarine and lapis lazuli.

Though gems are found all over the world, some regions are renowned for the quality and quantity of their minerals. For example, Minas Gerais in Brazil and Mogok in Myanmar (formerly Burma) produce a rich variety of gems, while the finest emeralds are found in Columbia.

AUSTRALIAN JEWELS Raw opal, from the Mintabie opal field in South Australia, on a piece of sandstone, its host rock. The eye-catching interplay of different colours in opal can be seen in the large piece above.

Opals

From the Latin *opalus*, meaning 'precious stone', opal is one of the few non-crystalline gems. It is a hardened silica gel that has been deposited in the fissures of many types of rock. Opal is commonly found in sedimentary rock, although it also occurs in cavities in volcanic rocks. It is an intriguing stone – it has all the colours of the rainbow, but the colours change depending on the angle of

OPAL OASIS *Little of Coober Pedy, Australia's unusual opal-mining town, can be seen above ground. To escape temperatures that soar to 45°C, the town's 3500 inhabitants live in cave-like dwellings underground, where they have also built an ornate church.*

viewing. It is as if the stone is alive, shifting and changing in a vibrant play of light. This unusual and attractive quality comes from the gem's internal structure: minute, uniformly sized silica spheres that reflect and disperse the light. Opal also contains water molecules trapped between the spheres, sometimes up to 10 per cent. Because of this opals can sometimes crack or even disintegrate as they dry out.

Precious opal is found in Brazil, Mexico and the USA, but by far the world's biggest producer is Australia with a lion's share of around 97 per cent. Rare black opals – which are actually very dark grey or blue – are found only at Lightning Ridge in New South Wales, while white opals are mined at Coober Pedy in

South Australia. Now the opal capital of the world, opals were first discovered in Coober Pedy in 1915. The name derives from the Aboriginal term *kupa piti*, which means 'white man in a hole'. The name is appropriate, because in order to survive the harsh, desert climate, miners excavated an underground town.

Opal gems are sold as solid cabochons, doublets or triplets. A cabochon is a gemstone that has been shaped – usually as an oval – and polished. In a doublet, a thin slice of darker coloured silica is cemented beneath a thin veneer of fine opal to enhance its colour, while a triplet has an additional thin layer of quartz placed over the top to protect the stone.

Rubies and sapphires

Both rubies and sapphires are forms of the mineral corundum, an aluminium oxide that is second only to diamond in its hardness, making the gems highly durable. Since corundum is naturally clear, the colour of a particular gem depends on any impurities that are present. Chromium produces the red coloration associated with rubies, while iron and titanium produce a deep blue colour typical of sapphires. The finest rubies come from Myanmar (Burma), where the intense colour of the stones has been described as 'pigeon's blood'. All natural rubies have

SYMBOL OF PASSION Ruby crystals are embedded in metamorphic gneiss. A ruby without any needle-like rutile inclusions indicates that the stone has been treated in some way.

imperfections in them, including colour impurities and inclusions of rutile (titanium dioxide) needles known as 'silk'. Sometimes the fine rutile needles cause the appearance of a six-rayed star effect when light catches the stone, a phenomenon known as asterism.

The finest sapphires come from Kashmir and Myanmar. Kashmir sapphires are a beautiful cornflower blue, those from Myanmar are bright, royal blue. Darker stones come from Thailand and Australia. Sapphires can also be pink, green, yellow and purple. As with rubies, sapphires can display a beautiful star-shaped pattern when light is reflected off the stone's needle-like inclusions.

Found in the gem gravels of Sri Lanka, padparadscha is a very rare and expensive form of corundum. The name in Sinhalese means 'lotus flower', describing the gem's pinkish-orange hue.

Emeralds

Traces of chromium and vanadium impart the velvety green colour of emerald, a form of the mineral beryl. It is very rare to find an emerald without a flaw; the brittle stones usually contain fractures and mineral inclusions. It is considered accepted practice to oil stones, often with cedar oil, to fill in any cracks and enhance the colour. The step cut (also known as the 'emerald cut') was designed to show off these stones to maximum effect. The finest emeralds are a strong green with a hint of blue. They are found in mines around Muzo and Chivor in Colombia, where they have formed veins in shales and limestones. One highly prized Colombian emerald is known as the trapiche – named after a grinding wheel – which exhibits a star pattern formed by dark inclusions that radiate like the spokes of a wheel from a central hexagonal core. Other sources of emerald include Brazil, Zambia, Zimbabwe, Madagascar, India, Pakistan, Afghanistan and Russia.

Two of the largest uncut stones are the Devonshire and the Patricia. The 1383-carat Devonshire emerald is a hexagonal crystal about 5 cm wide and 6 cm tall. It was found in the Muzo mine in Colombia. It was given to the sixth Duke of Devonshire by Emperor Dom Pedro of Brazil in 1831. The Patricia is another exquisite Colombian emerald that is now on display at the American Museum of Natural History. It was found in the Chivor mine in 1920 and named after the mine owner's daughter. The deep-green, 632-carat gem is unusual in that it has 12 sides.

Even larger emeralds have been reported in antiquity, including an enormous obelisk in the Egyptian temple of Amun. It was reputedly made of four rows of emeralds and was roughly 18 m tall and 1.5 m wide. If such an amazing object did exist, the

EMERALD CRYSTALS
This specimen, measuring 10 x 8 cm, was found at a mine in north-east Brazil.

CRYSTAL CLUSTER Spanish geologists inside what is believed to be the world's largest crystal cluster. Situated in Almeria in southern Spain, the underground cavity is resplendent with gypsum prisms.

emeralds are likely to have come from Queen Cleopatra's mines, the source of some of the finest emeralds in the ancient world.

Amber and jet

Formed millions of years ago when dinosaurs roamed the Earth, amber is a remarkable material, providing a unique time-capsule of the prehistoric world. It is formed from sticky resin which oozed from ancient pine trees. Over time, the resin became encased in dirt and debris, and eventually it fossilised. Sometimes insects, mushrooms, plant material, feathers and even small amimals, such as tiny tree-living frogs, became entrapped in the resin and they, too, were fossilised. The result is that some important fossils have been found in deposits of amber, including the world's oldest known bee, discovered in New Jersey, USA, and preserved for some 65 to 80 million years.

Amber can be transparent or opaque in many shades of yellow and orange. It has a smooth, warm, soft texture. It is also very light for its size, making it ideal for jewellery. Amber increases in value with the rarity and perfection of the entrapped object. Though amber can be found all over the world, the most significant resource is the Baltic coasts of Russia and Poland, where it has been collected from beaches and traded for thousands of years. Sometimes Baltic amber washes up on beaches in eastern Britain. True amber can be distinguished from brown glass – and from fake man-made amber produced from plastic resins – because it floats in salty water. Another good source of amber is the Dominican Republic. This amber is younger and slightly softer in texture than Baltic amber and can sometimes be deep red, green or even blue in colour.

Amber-like copal is a semi-fossilised resin used as an incense by indigenous peoples of Mexico and Central America. It is sometimes substituted for amber in jewellery.

Jet is another fossilised material that has long been treated as a gemstone. Black or dark brown in colour, it is fossilised wood, a hard type of lignite coal, 100 million years old. It can be cut and polished to an attractive lustre and has been used for jewellery for thousands of years – items of jet have been found in ancient burial sites. Its popularity soared in Britain in the 19th century after Queen Victoria started to wear it as part of her mourning dress following the death of Prince Albert in 1861. Jet is found in Spain, Turkey, the USA and Russia, but the largest deposits are at Whitby on England's north-east coast, where it has been mined since prehistoric times.

FACTS THE STAR OF INDIA IS THE LARGEST AND MOST FAMOUS STAR sapphire in the world. The 563-carat gem was discovered over 300 years ago in Sri Lanka. It is almost flawless and, unusually, has stars on both sides of the stone.

POLISHED SPHERES of rock crystal (quartz) have been used since Greek and Roman times for 'crystal gazing'.

ABORIGINES BELIEVE THE OPAL represents something an ancestor left behind as a sign of his or her presence. **FACTS**

STRENGTH

STREN

TO
GTH

6

SOMETIMES CALLED THE 'BIRD'S NEST' BECAUSE OF ITS UNUSUAL WOVEN LATTICE STRUCTURE, Beijing's Olympic stadium (left), built to house the opening and closing ceremonies of the 2008 games, is steel technology become a work of art. The 100 000-seat stadium incorporates an astonishing 45 000 tonnes of steel in the form of enormous hollow, box-shaped girders that wrap around the structure without a right angle in sight. Steel technology has long been an indicator of economic prowess. In the modern world, as more metals have been discovered and metallurgical technology has become more sophisticated, all manner of complex alloys have been created, with greater strength, flexibility and durability. The result is that today even the wildest dreams of an architect can often be realised.

METAL ORES

THE NARROW, RUGGED VALLEY OF THE QUEBRADA DE HUMAHUACA IN ARGENTINA'S JUJUY PROVINCE IS A PLACE OF MANY COLOURS. It cuts through the dry Andean foothills, which spread out like multicoloured waves. They are particularly striking around the village of Purmamarca, which shelters under the Cerro de los Siete Colores (Hill of the Seven Colours). The landscape's dramatic spectrum of hues is a result of the varied minerals in its rocks.

Each colour represents a different sedimentary deposit, and each deposit – laid down during a different period of geological time, from the Precambrian to the Quaternary – contains different minerals. The oldest pigments are green copper oxides from 600 million years ago. Then come off-white limestones, about 400 million years old. Following these are rocks dating from 80–90 million years ago, coloured

ELEMENTARY CLUES Violets, rusty reds, yellows, browns and white are among the many hues that colour the Quebrada de Humahuaca valley in north-western Argentina. The different tints indicate different elements in the rock – violet for lead, red for iron, yellow for sulphur, brown for manganese, white for calcium.

mustard-yellow by sulphur and violet by lead. Reddish hues mark out clays, sandstones and mudstones containing iron oxides – these were laid down 3–4 million years ago. Finally, a band of brown rock, a mere 1–2 million years old, contains manganese. Due to erosion and other geological processes, the layers have been mixed up in places, so they don't always appear in chronological order. The mingling only adds to the drama of the spectacle.

No doubt, the coloured rocks inspired the prehistoric artists who created the cave paintings that have been found in the region – they would almost certainly have provided the pigments for the paintings. The 150 km valley, carved out by the Río Grande, has long been an important cultural and trade route,

sometimes called the Camino Inca (the Inca Way, after the Inca empire). The artwork and other archaeological evidence point to human habitation going back 10 000 years.

Formation of ores

With the exception of the native metals such as gold and silver, which can be found in their pure state in nature, most metals occur only in combination with other elements. They form various minerals and ores, giving the Earth several of its colours. The striking reds of many desert rocks, for example, are usually due to the presence of iron oxides, while the greens in places such as northern Arizona's Painted Desert are due to copper compounds.

RICH DEPOSITS Iron ore is extracted from an open-pit mine at Carajás in north-eastern Brazil. The area also has significant deposits of manganese, gold, copper and aluminium ores.

Metal-containing minerals are called ores when they have enough metal to be worth extracting. The concentration needed varies, depending on a strictly human factor – the market price of a particular metal. Platinum is so valuable that a concentration of three parts per million in the rock is enough to make it worth exploiting. For iron, on the other hand, the rock needs to contain at least 50 per cent iron to count as an ore.

Metal ores arise because something has concentrated, transported and deposited the metallic element. There are a number of ways in which this can happen, and often an ore will have been formed by a succession of several processes. One common mechanism is the process in which hot, mineral-laden fluids travel up through fissures and faults in rock in the Earth's crust. On reaching a cooler region nearer the surface, the fluid cools or undergoes a chemical reaction to deposit the metallic element. Ores that are formed in this way include those of copper, lead, zinc, silver and gold.

Another type of ore is called a residual deposit, of which iron ore is an example. Weathering (see page 21) oxidises the iron minerals to form insoluble oxides and hydroxides, giving the soil or rock a characteristic red, brown, yellow or black coloration. Rainwater washes away any soluble minerals, so that the iron oxides and hydroxides become concentrated as a residue. Nickel and aluminium ores also form this way.

Another common type of ore is a placer deposit (placer, pronounced 'plass-er', comes from the Spanish for 'sandbank'). This occurs where the mineral has been concentrated by the movement of surface-flowing water. Famous examples of placer deposits include the gold found in or near streams and rivers by lucky prospectors during the gold rushes of the 19th and early 20th centuries. Non-metals can also be deposited in this way, such as the gems and diamonds sometimes found in gravel beds.

A PALETTE OF PIGMENTS

LONG BEFORE METAL ORES WERE USED TO EXTRACT METALS, HUMANS TOOK ADVANTAGE OF THE COLOURFUL MINERALS TO PAINT THEIR BODIES AND THE WALLS OF CAVES. In 1940, four teenage boys stumbled across cave paintings, even older than

SHADES OF OCHRE Iron oxides in the clay around Roussillon in France colour the soil ochre red and yellow. Ochre pigments quarried here are regarded as the best in the world.

those of the Quebrada de Humahuaca, in Lascaux in southern France. Some 30 000 years after their Palaeolithic artists had drawn them, the paintings still vividly depicted large red bulls, yellow horses and black stags. The only pigments available would have been the clays and minerals found locally.

The earliest pigments used in prehistoric times included iron oxides, which provided reddish colours, and manganese oxides, which gave brownish and blackish hues. Clay earths, such as ochres and siennas, would also have been used, providing shades of yellow and brown. In many cave paintings, although not those at Lascaux, carbon from burnt wood (charcoal) or ivory was used as the black pigment. The pigments were ground into a fine powder and added to a binding matrix, such as water, urine, animal fats, blood or egg white. They were applied with a twig or finger.

Colours from far-off places

Natural earth and mineral pigments continued to be used for fine art until chemists began to formulate synthetic replacements, starting in the 18th century. Pigments were often traded over great distances and would frequently be named after the area where they were found. They included raw and burnt sienna, from Siena in Italy, and umber, from Umbria. Persian red came from the island of Ormuz in the Persian Gulf.

Some commanded extraordinarily high prices, because they were very rare or mined in remote regions. One was ultramarine, a blue pigment that was more valuable than gold during the Renaissance. It is made from lapis lazuli or, more precisely, the mineral lazurite within it. At the time, lapis lazuli was available only from Afghanistan. If a patron wanted a painter to use ultramarine in a portrait, he had to sign an agreement to reimburse the artist for the extra cost involved. In illuminated manuscripts and other forms of religious art, the highest-quality ultramarine was reserved for painting the robes of Christ and the Virgin Mary. Chemists put much effort into finding a substitute for the expensive ultramarine, but it was not until the early 19th century that a perfect synthetic form was created, known as French ultramarine.

Poisonous paints

Many of the earliest pigments were poisonous, because they contained arsenic, lead and mercury-based minerals. But just as some modern women undergo botox injections and cosmetic surgery, women in medieval times and later were prepared to suffer in the pursuit of beauty.

In Elizabethan England a pale complexion indicated high status – it meant that a person did not do manual work in the fields. Women kept their skin pale by avoiding the Sun and by painting their faces with whitening mixtures, including a mixture of vinegar

PIGMENTS AND COLOURS

Today, a range of synthetic pigments have joined the natural ones. A German painter, Heinrich Diesbach, accidentally created the first synthetic pigment, Prussian blue, in 1704, when he used potash (potassium carbonate) tainted with animal oil while trying to mix a red pigment.

METAL	PIGMENTS
Antimony	Antimony white
Arsenic	Paris green, realgar (red), orpiment (yellow)
Cadmium	Cadmium red, yellow & orange
Chromium	Chrome green, chrome yellow, viridian (green)
Cobalt	Cobalt blue, green & violet, cerulean blue, aureolin (yellow)
Copper	Azurite (blue), Egyptian blue, malachite (green), verdigris (green)
Iron	Caput mortuum (purple), brown, yellow & red ochre, Venetian red, Mars black, Prussian blue, raw & burnt sienna
Lead	Lead white, Naples yellow, red & blue lead
Mercury	Vermilion red
Titanium	Titanium white, yellow & black

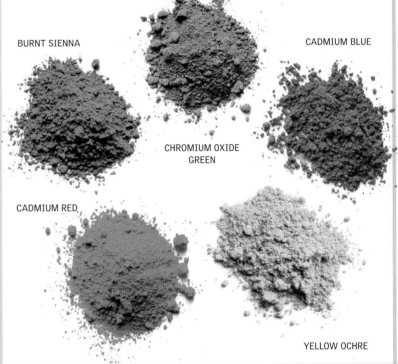

BURNT SIENNA

CADMIUM BLUE

CHROMIUM OXIDE GREEN

CADMIUM RED

YELLOW OCHRE

and ceruse (powdered white lead). They also used a red dye made from mercury sulphide for their lips and rouge for their cheeks made from red ochre in a lead base. The painted face would be preserved in a coating of egg-white. The application of lead and mercury-based products meant that many women felt the effects of heavy-metal poisoning. A high forehead became fashionable, as seen in many of Queen Elizabeth I's portraits, and this may in part have been due to the loss of hair from lead poisoning. A process called enamelling, in which a coating of lead-based whitener was applied over a lady's face and neck, lasted into the 19th century, when it fell out of favour during the Victorian era. Today, poisonous pigments are still used, but only in some artists' paints.

THE AGE OF ALLOYS

NO ONE KNOWS WHO FIRST MIXED COPPER WITH TIN TO MAKE BRONZE. It could have been an accident, since tin ore sometimes occurs alongside copper ore. Perhaps an ancient metalworker noticed that when copper contained impurities of tin, it produced a metal that was much harder and more durable than pure copper. Whatever the case, we know that people have been making things out of bronze since around 3500 BC – marking the start of the Bronze Age.

The technology to make this alloy – a material composed of two or more metals or a metal and a non-metal – appears to have started with the Mesopotamians in the ancient Middle East. From there it spread slowly westwards across Europe, reaching Britain by about 1800 BC. The ability to make bronze gave cultures a huge advantage. It is much harder than copper and enabled people to construct stronger weapons, armour and tools. Moreover, bronze has a lower melting point than copper and so is suitable for casting, the process in which molten metal is poured into a mould and allowed to harden. This makes it very versatile in its applications.

Combined properties

The advantage of an alloy is that it can combine the most useful properties of two or more different materials. Nowadays, the range of metal alloys available to us is vast and ever more sophisticated. Yet bronze, the most ancient of them all, retains its place

Bronze, the most ancient of alloys, retains its place as the best material for many uses, from ships' propellers to engine bearings to statuary.

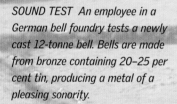

SOUND TEST An employee in a German bell foundry tests a newly cast 12-tonne bell. Bells are made from bronze containing 20–25 per cent tin, producing a metal of a pleasing sonority.

as the best material for many uses, from ships' propellers to engine bearings to statuary, often with small amounts of other metals added to the copper and tin to impart particular properties.

Bronze with 0.5 per cent phosphorus, for example, is particularly robust – 'phosphor bronze' is used where strength and resistance to corrosion are important, as in ships' propellers, pumps, precision bearings and springs. Sometimes, other metals are used in the alloy instead of tin. Aluminium bronzes contain up to 10 per cent aluminium and may contain silicon, manganese, iron and zinc – lightweight and strong, they are used in engine parts.

In statuary, bronze is still the preferred metal for most sculptors, for its physical as well as its aesthetic properties. Typically, the bronze used in statues has 10 per cent tin, along with a little zinc to give it extra strength. It is easy to cast in a mould, strong and ductile – meaning that it can be drawn out into a long, thin shape (as in the limbs of a human figure) without readily breaking. One other valuable attribute is that cast bronze expands slightly as it sets. For sculptors, this means that finished bronzes will faithfully replicate even the most precise details of their moulds.

Another ancient art made possible by bronze and continuing today much as it has done for centuries is bell founding. Bells are cast in moulds comprised of an inner 'core' and an outer 'cope'. The space between the two parts is the desired shape of the bell. Before pouring in the molten bronze, the mould is packed in damp sand to prevent rapid cooling of the metal – large bells may take up to two weeks to cool. Once set, the bell is sandblasted and polished. It may then be tuned by removing small amounts of metal until it reaches the desired pitch. Traditionally, bells with their unique, sonorous 'voices' were given names, many of which survive to this day, such as Big Ben in London's Palace of Westminster, Little John in Nottingham's

Council House, Decke Pitter (Fat Peter) and Maria Gloriosa in the German cathedrals of Cologne and Erfurt and Zygmunt (or Big Sig) in Wawel Cathedral in Krakow, Poland.

Polished brasses

Other traditional alloys made with copper include brass, pewter and nickel silver. Brass is typically 90 per cent copper and 10 per cent zinc. Today, it is mostly used in musical instruments and in decorative metalwork – horse brasses are a popular use for the attractive yellow alloy, which can be given a fine polish. It was often used in early precision instruments, such as telescopes.

Pewter is like the inverse of bronze – tin alloyed with between 1 and 15 per cent copper to give it more strength. In Europe, most plates and drinking vessels were made from pewter until china and glass became cheaper to manufacture in the 18th and 19th centuries. It is too malleable to be good for making tools, but this same quality makes it easy to carve or punch impressions into for decorative tableware.

Nickel silver is a silvery-coloured alloy of copper with nickel and sometimes zinc. It was made in China until German metalworkers in the 19th century succeeded in replicating it – hence its other name, German silver. It is often used as a base metal for silver-plated cutlery – such as EPNS (electroplated nickel silver) ware – and in zips, musical instruments and the coins of some currencies, such as the US 5 cent piece, commonly called a 'nickel'.

CORNISH TIN Cornwall was a major source of tin during the Bronze Age, and traders came from all over Europe and the Mediterranean to buy it there. These old engine houses at Bosigran near St Ives are lonely witnesses to an industry that continued into the late 20th century.

METAL FROM SPACE

IRON IS THE SECOND MOST COMMON METAL IN THE EARTH'S CRUST AND THE FOURTH MOST COMMON ELEMENT. Yet in nature it is only ever encountered in its pure metallic state in meteorites, which have crashed into the Earth from outer space. Otherwise, it exists on our planet only as an ore in combination with other elements.

For ancient peoples, who had not yet learned how to extract metals from ores, meteorites were the only source of iron. Falling all over the Earth at random, the iron-bearing meteorites must have seemed like celestial gifts, which is why the ancient Egyptians called iron the 'metal of heaven'. The oldest-known iron objects – 6000-year-old beads found in Egypt – were made from meteoritic iron. People broke meteorites up and hammered out the iron to make small decorative objects, such as beads, or to use on the tips of spears.

NIGHT LIGHTS Every year in mid November, the night skies sparkle with shooting stars during the so-called Leonid shower. It happens when the Earth's orbit takes it through a stream of particles left by the passage of the comet Tempel-Tuttle.

Hitting the atmosphere

Every day, around 100 tonnes of extraterrestrial material falls to Earth. Most of it arrives as dust grains less than 1 mm across that burn up on entering the atmosphere – we see the grains as shooting stars. Objects large enough to make it through the atmosphere occur less frequently – about 1000 of them, weighing anything between 1 and 100 kg, do so every year. These meteorites are divided into three main types: stones (composed of minerals also often found in rocks on Earth), irons (composed of iron metal alloyed with nickel) and stony irons (a mixture of stone and metal). Most meteorites are stones; iron-bearing ones make up only 5 per cent of the total.

Although the distribution of meteorites across the planet is fairly even, there are certain places where they are more commonly found than in others because the natural environment has helped to preserve or concentrate them. In arid climates, meteorites are less likely to deteriorate through rusting than in humid conditions, so deserts (hot or cold) are good places for finding them. In their parched conditions, the meteorites can stay intact for thousands of years, and their numbers build up over time. Significant numbers of meteorites have been found, for example, in the Dar al Gani, Hammadah al Hamra and Adra regions of the Sahara, the Nullarbor Plain in South and Western Australia, the Namib Desert in south-western Africa and the Atacama Desert in Chile.

The record, however, goes to the appropriately named Meteorite Hills of Antarctica, which have the world's highest concentration of meteorites. A group of Japanese geologists discovered the first

ones in 1969, and since then tens of thousands of others have been recovered from the region – more than all the other finds on Earth put together. One reason for this abundance in Antarctica is that the movement of glaciers has concentrated the meteorites. When a mountain stands in the path of a glacier, the glacier continues to pile into it, carrying a cargo of rocks and meteorites, which grow in number.

Today, scientists still value these arrivals from space – but not as our ancestors did, as a possible source of iron. They study the structure and composition of meteorites to gain a greater understanding of the Solar System and its origins – their composition gives clues about the changing conditions as the Solar System was formed. Some also contain dust and chemicals that were produced by stars before the solar system was even formed, giving an insight into the history of the entire universe. In addition, meteorite impacts have had a very direct influence on the shaping of the Earth itself and life on Earth. A large impact may have been responsible for the formation of the Moon, for example. Another impact 65 million years ago is believed to have led to the extinction of the dinosaurs.

IRON MONSTER The 60 tonne Hoba meteorite (left) in Namibia smashed into the Earth more than 80 000 years ago. It is the world's heaviest meteorite, composed of 84 per cent iron alloyed with nickel and some cobalt.

METEORITIC SPARKLE Found in Chile's Atacama Desert, this stony-iron meteorite (right) is a pallasite, with a distinctive crystalline structure.

AGE OF IRON

SMELTING IRON FROM ITS OXIDE ORES IS A RELATIVELY STRAIGHTFORWARD PROCESS. **Workers only need to heat the ore with carbon (in the form of charcoal), and the products will be iron and carbon dioxide.** Adding limestone helps, as it takes out impurities. The limestone decomposes in the heat to form quicklime (calcium oxide), which combines with the impurities (mainly silicates) to form a slag that can be easily removed.

Learning how to do this was one of the key discoveries of ancient societies, inaugurating the Iron Age. Iron represented an advance on bronze, because iron weapons were harder and lighter than bronze ones. And there was plenty of raw material to make them from. Unlike the tin ore needed to make bronze, iron ore is abundant worldwide.

Wrought, cast and pig

Before the invention of blast furnaces, iron was produced in small forges, known as bloomeries, which couldn't reach high enough temperatures to separate the iron fully. The end product was a mass of iron and slag, called a bloom. This had to be reheated, then hammered repeatedly and worked (or 'wrought') to remove the slag. The method was time-consuming, but the wrought iron was flexible and easily shaped.

To melt iron so that it can be poured into moulds ('cast') requires much hotter furnaces. The Chinese were using such furnaces from around 600 BC, but these did not reach Europe until about the 14th century AD. Known as blast furnaces, because of the blast of hot air blown through them with bellows, they produced molten iron that could be cast into ingots, called 'pigs'. In 1709, Abraham Darby, an ironmaster at Coalbrookdale in Shropshire, started to fuel his blast furnaces with coke instead of charcoal. Coke is made

NATURAL MAGNETISM Iron is a ferromagnetic material – it becomes magnetised when placed in a magnetic field and stays magnetised for a period of time afterwards. One of its ores, magnetite or lodestone, was used in early magnetic compasses.

SWORD OF CEREMONY This wrought-iron ceremonial sword with a brass pommel was made in Spain in the 14th century, while the country was under Muslim Moorish rule.

by burning off excess moisture from low-sulphur bituminous coal (see pages 58–59) in the absence of air, and it produces the high temperatures needed in blast furnaces, making the process cheaper and more efficient.

The modern smelting process is essentially the same. Coke, iron ore and fluxes (minerals such as limestone or dolomite that remove impurities) are fed into the top of a blast furnace. Hot air (at about 1200°C) blasts in at the bottom and ignites the coke, which produces carbon monoxide as it burns. The carbon monoxide reacts with the iron ore to produce molten iron and carbon dioxide, and the fluxes form a slag. The molten iron sinks to the bottom of the furnace, with the slag floating on top. Taps at the side allow the molten iron and slag to drain off. The pig iron can be further purified or used to make steel.

THE WORLD'S BIGGEST EXPORTERS OF IRON ORE

FACTS are Australia and Brazil, each contributing about a third of total exports. India, China and Russia are also key producers. According to the US Geological Survey, around 1500 million tonnes of iron ore were extracted in 2005. Today, almost all iron ore (98 per cent) is used for making steel.

ANATOLIA WAS ONE OF THE FIRST

TO SMELT A TONNE of pig iron from an ore with 60 per cent iron requires around 250 kg of limestone flux and a tonne of coke.

places in which iron was smelted, around 1300 BC.

FACTS

HAMMERING OUT Traditionally, horseshoes were made from tough, malleable wrought iron. Nowadays, they are generally made from steel, as is most ornamental 'wrought iron' work, such as railings.

STEEL IS THE WORLD'S MOST USEFUL STRUCTURAL METAL – RELATIVELY CHEAP TO PRODUCE, STRONG AND LESS CORROSIVE THAN IRON. It makes trains, ships, cars and tools. From skyscrapers to suspension bridges, many of the modern world's iconic structures would be impossible without steel – 3000 km of steel cables were used, for example, in the world's longest suspension bridge, the Akashi-Kaikyo in Japan.

The discovery of steel happened because ironworkers were using charcoal (containing carbon) in their smelting furnaces. Normally, this produced pig iron, containing 3.5 per cent carbon. But sometimes, if the carbon content was reduced to 0.3–1.2 per cent, a hard but pliable alloy emerged. In just the right amount, carbon imparts great strength and ductility. The resulting steel can also be 'tempered' to make it harder. It is heated to a high temperature, then cooled rapidly in water or oil to trap the carbon atoms in an extremely hard crystalline structure called martensite. After that, it is heated again and cooled slowly to reduce brittleness. Today, steelmaking is one of the world's most important industries. In 2005, 1100 million tonnes of steel were produced, more than a third of this in China.

An ancient skill

Steel was already known in ancient times. It was being made in East Africa as early as 1400 BC and in China by the 1st century AD. The skills of Asian steel-makers can be seen in the impressive samurai swords, wrought in Japan from the 10th century onwards. They are so sharp that if a feather falls on the blade, it will, literally, be cut in two. In Europe, the Spanish city of Toledo was renowned for its finely crafted steel swords.

It wasn't until 1855, however, that a process was devised that enabled manufacturers to produce steel reliably in large amounts. Named the Bessemer process after its inventor, the English engineer Henry Bessemer, the new process relied on compressed air blasting through molten pig iron to remove most of the carbon and other impurities. The process took place in a huge vessel called a Bessemer converter. As the air shot up through the molten liquid, a fountain of sparks and flames poured out of the top of the vessel. With experience, it was possible to judge whether the process was complete from the colour and size of the flames. Today, most steel is manufactured by the basic oxygen process, essentially the same as the Bessemer process except that it uses pure oxygen instead of air.

Steel technology is now highly advanced, and steels can be made with countless special properties to increase their hardness, strength when stretched (tensile strength), ductility and malleability. This is done by processes such as heat treatment (tempering) and by alloying iron with other metals including vanadium, tungsten, manganese and molybdenum. Stainless steels, for example, contain a minimum of 10 per cent chromium and sometimes have nickel as well to increase their resistance to corrosion. Tool steels, used for equipment such as drills and axes, are hardened by heat treatment and contain tungsten and cobalt, which makes them more resistant to high temperatures.

STEEL

FIRE FOUNTAIN The sparks fly in a US steel foundry, manufacturing rails for railways. Until the invention of the Bessemer process, steel could only be made in relatively small quantities. Its use was mostly confined to blades of various kinds and springs for clocks and watches.

GLASS AND STEEL A lattice of steel supports the glass walls of Seattle's Central Library, opened in May 2004. More than 4600 tonnes of steel were used, enough to make 20 Statues of Liberty.

MODERN METALS

WHEN ALUMINIUM WAS FIRST PRODUCED IN THE 19TH CENTURY, IT WAS MORE PRECIOUS THAN GOLD. Emperor Napoleon III of France is said to have had plates and dishes made of it, such was the silvery metal's cachet. Aluminium remained a luxury until a Frenchman, Paul Héroult, and an American, Charles M. Hall, independently developed a relatively cheap way of extracting it in 1886. Since then, it has gone from being a luxury metal to one of the most important materials on Earth.

Many of the things we take for granted in modern life would be unthinkable without aluminium, along with the range of other metals and alloys we now have at our disposal. While steel is a vital structural material, it is comparatively heavy. More recently discovered metals, notably aluminium and titanium, offer strength with lightness, a combination that has proved invaluable in planes and cars, for example. By mixing aluminium or titanium with small amounts of other metals, metallurgists have also created a spectrum of alloys, offering specific properties for particular tasks.

As well as being light and strong, aluminium is extremely malleable (only gold is more so), which means that it can be formed into all sorts of useful shapes. It is also very resistant to corrosion.

RICH RED EARTH The world's largest bauxite mine is at Weipa in Queensland, Australia. From there, the ore is taken to Gladstone, Queensland, where it is processed, using electricity from coal-fired generating stations – the region has rich coal deposits. Although Australia is the world's largest producer of bauxite, China is the largest producer of processed aluminium, followed by Russia, Canada and the USA.

Attributes of aluminium

For engineers, aluminium has countless valuable properties. As well as being light and strong, it is extremely malleable (only gold is more so), which means that it can be formed into all sorts of useful shapes. It is also very resistant to corrosion, because it reacts with oxygen in the air to form a thin layer of aluminium oxide over the surface of the metal – scratch a piece of aluminium, and the metal 'heals' itself as a layer of oxide forms to fill in the gap. Its common uses range from drinks cans to electrical wiring to most forms of transport. It is vital in the aerospace industry, which is constantly developing new aluminium alloys in its quest to reduce weight while maintaining strength – a 1 per cent reduction in an aircraft's weight can bring massive savings in fuel costs.

Fortunately for us, this important metal is abundant. It is the most common metal on Earth, composing 8 per cent of our planet's crust, and the third most common element after silicon and oxygen. More tricky is the fact that large deposits of its major ore, bauxite, the source of 99 per cent of the aluminium in use, are found only in a relatively few places. Bauxite is a residual deposit (see page 124), formed by chemical weathering of aluminium-rich rocks, usually in a tropical climate. The world's largest producer is Australia, accounting for more than 40 per cent of the global production of bauxite, followed by Brazil, Guinea and Jamaica.

Another difficulty is with the process of extracting the aluminium from the bauxite, first developed by Hall and Héroult, which involves electrolysis. This means that it requires large amounts of electricity. In the Hall-Héroult process, the ore is dissolved in molten cryolite (sodium aluminium fluoride), and then an electric current is passed through the liquid. When this happens, the aluminium precipitates at the cathode (positive electrode), while carbon dioxide bubbles up at the anode (negative electrode). The aluminium is denser than the cryolite in which it was dissolved, and so sinks to the bottom of the chamber, where it can be tapped off as pure molten metal. Because of the need for so much electricity, aluminium processing often takes place near hydroelectric power plants, far from the region where the bauxite was mined.

A vicar's discovery

An Anglican clergyman and keen amateur geologist first discovered the modern world's other 'wonder' metal, titanium. The Revd William Gregor was a vicar in Cornwall, when he made his find in a stream near his parish in 1791. A few years later, a German chemist, Martin Klaproth, made another find, in Hungary, and named it after the Titan gods of Greek mythology. Nowadays, the aerospace industry is the largest user of the metal and its alloys. Since it is expensive, however, it tends to be used more selectively than aluminium alloys in plane parts.

LIGHT STRENGTH Aluminium's strength, lightness and resistance to corrosion make it ideal for installations such as these escalators at London Bridge station on the London Underground.

TITANIUM

A HIGH STRENGTH-TO-WEIGHT RATIO

IS TITANIUM'S GREAT VIRTUE AS A METAL. Tungsten, for example, is harder – measuring 7.5 on Mohs scale of hardness (see page 153) – but its density is 19 250 kg per m³. Titanium, with a slightly lower Mohs hardness of 6.0, is almost five times lighter. It is also inert (it reacts chemically only under extreme conditions) and has a high resistance to corrosion and heat, which explains why it has become a key material in our technological age, its uses ranging from hip replacements to spacecraft, jewellery to household paint.

In Bilbao, Spain, the Guggenheim Museum (below) displays its lustrous titanium fish-scale coating to stunning effect. But you are as likely to find titanium in the home. The whiteness and opacity of titanium oxide make it the most widely used inorganic paint pigment – from apple white to magnolia, most paints contain it. It has many applications in spacecraft, especially when alloyed with aluminium, vanadium, iron or molybdenum. It is also biocompatible, which means that it can be used in the human body for implants such as hip replacements, heart valves and pacemakers without causing problematic side-effects.

CHEMICAL SYMBOL Ti
ATOMIC NUMBER 22
TYPE OF ELEMENT Transition metal
APPEARANCE Silvery grey metal
DENSITY 4510 kg/m³
MELTING POINT 1667°C
ORES The most important are the minerals ilmenite, leucoxene and rutile.
PRODUCTION Australia is the world's biggest producer of titanium ore.

VITAL STATISTICS

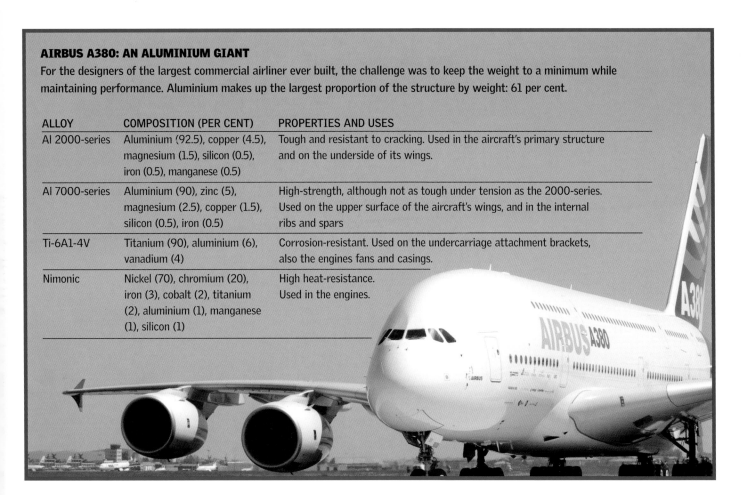

AIRBUS A380: AN ALUMINIUM GIANT

For the designers of the largest commercial airliner ever built, the challenge was to keep the weight to a minimum while maintaining performance. Aluminium makes up the largest proportion of the structure by weight: 61 per cent.

ALLOY	COMPOSITION (PER CENT)	PROPERTIES AND USES
Al 2000-series	Aluminium (92.5), copper (4.5), magnesium (1.5), silicon (0.5), iron (0.5), manganese (0.5)	Tough and resistant to cracking. Used in the aircraft's primary structure and on the underside of its wings.
Al 7000-series	Aluminium (90), zinc (5), magnesium (2.5), copper (1.5), silicon (0.5), iron (0.5)	High-strength, although not as tough under tension as the 2000-series. Used on the upper surface of the aircraft's wings, and in the internal ribs and spars
Ti-6A1-4V	Titanium (90), aluminium (6), vanadium (4)	Corrosion-resistant. Used on the undercarriage attachment brackets, also the engines fans and casings.
Nimonic	Nickel (70), chromium (20), iron (3), cobalt (2), titanium (2), aluminium (1), manganese (1), silicon (1)	High heat-resistance. Used in the engines.

In ancient Greek mythology, the Titans were overthrown as gods and imprisoned underground. It is an appropriate analogy for the metal named after them, since it is remarkably difficult to liberate from its ores, even though these are numerous and titanium is abundant in the Earth's crust. This explains why it was not commercially produced until the late 1940s, after a method for reducing the ore with magnesium had been developed – called the Kroll process, after its inventor, the Luxembourg-born metallurgist William Kroll. Large-scale production arrived in time for the space race, and titanium was used in the *Apollo* rockets. The space shuttles also have titanium parts, as does the International Space Station.

Metallic glasses

Imagine a metal with the elasticity of plastic and twice the strength of titanium. It now exists in the form of the metallic glasses – materials such as Liquidmetal, developed by scientists working in the USA. Traditionally, solid metals or alloys, such as steel, aluminium and titanium, have an orderly structure, where the atoms are locked together in a number of repeating units or cells. But the metallic glasses are different, and therein lies the secret of their unusual properties – their molecular structure is more disorganised, like that of a liquid.

To achieve this 'amorphous' configuration, metals are heated to a molten state, where the atoms can move about freely. If the molten alloy is then supercooled very quickly,

the atoms do not have time to revert to their preferred orderly structure. It is as though they are 'frozen' in a disordered arrangement. The difficulty is that supercooling an alloy is usually costly and hard to achieve. Using a complex blend of zirconium, titanium, nickel, copper and beryllium, however, American scientists created an alloy that turns from a liquid to a glassy solid at room temperature. The first use of this extraordinary material has been in sports equipment, such as golf clubs, tennis rackets and baseballs, in which the light, elastic metallic glass transfers more energy from the player to the ball.

WAY AHEAD Metallic glasses such as Liquidmetal (above), developed by scientists at NASA, the US Department of Energy and the California Institute of Technology, combine elasticity, strength and resistance to corrosion.

RECYCLING
METALS

THERE IS A LARGE AND WELL-DEFINED MARKET IN THE RECYCLING OF METALS, SINCE IN MOST CASES IT IS FAR CHEAPER THAN PROCESSING THE METALS FROM THEIR ORES. The cost of recycling aluminium, for example, is just 5 per cent of the cost of extracting it from its ore, bauxite. By recycling steel, manufacturers may save themselves 75 per cent of the costs of making it from scratch. Recycling also helps to conserve our planet's valuable resources and energy. According to the UK-based Waste and Resources Action Programme (WRAP), recycling 1 kg of

aluminium saves 6 kg of bauxite, 4 kg of chemicals needed to process the bauxite and 14 kilowatts of electricity. The process also reduces emissions of carbon dioxide by 95 per cent.

In fact, aluminium is the most valuable of the commonly recycled materials. This is partly because of the sheer volume involved – the UK population alone gets through around 5 billion aluminium drinks cans each year – and partly because aluminium is particularly suitable for recycling. Reprocessing does not affect its structure so it can be recycled indefinitely. To do so, old cans are collected and shredded, with any coloured coating removed. Giant furnaces then melt down the shreds, and the molten metal is poured into massive slabs – about 1.6 million cans make one large ingot.

Steel scrap is also recycled in bulk. In 2004, scrap metal made up half the furnace feed for steel, coming

CRUSHED CANS Workers at a recycling plant examine bales of crushed aluminium drinks cans. Recycling is particularly important in the manufacture of aluminium, which is expensive to extract from its ore.

from packaging, old vehicles and construction waste, as well as the scrap generated by the process of steel manufacturing itself. This goes straight back into the foundry.

A computer gold mine

In the USA, up to 20 million personal computers become obsolete every year, yet three-quarters of them are not thrown out. In due course, most find their way to landfill sites, because their owners don't know how else to dispose of them. Such a supply could be a bonanza for recyclers.

Mining companies dig holes 4 km deep in the ground to extract gold ore. But computers, laptops, mobile phones and other electronic equipment represent a rich deposit much closer at hand. According to the US Geological Survey, 1 tonne of electronic scrap from personal computers contains on average more gold than would be recovered from 17 tonnes of gold ore. And there are other valuable materials in old electronics as well, including aluminium, barium, beryllium, copper, gallium, iron, manganese, palladium, platinum, silver and zinc. To retrieve them, the equipment is dismantled. The components that can be reused are sold, toxic elements removed and the metallic parts shredded and sorted. These are then sold as scrap and recycled in smelting plants. Although still underexploited, this is a potential gold mine

CIRCUIT BOARDS TO JEWELS A worker for the Swiss company Metalor sorts computer circuit boards for recycling (left). The gold extracted is used by some of the world's most

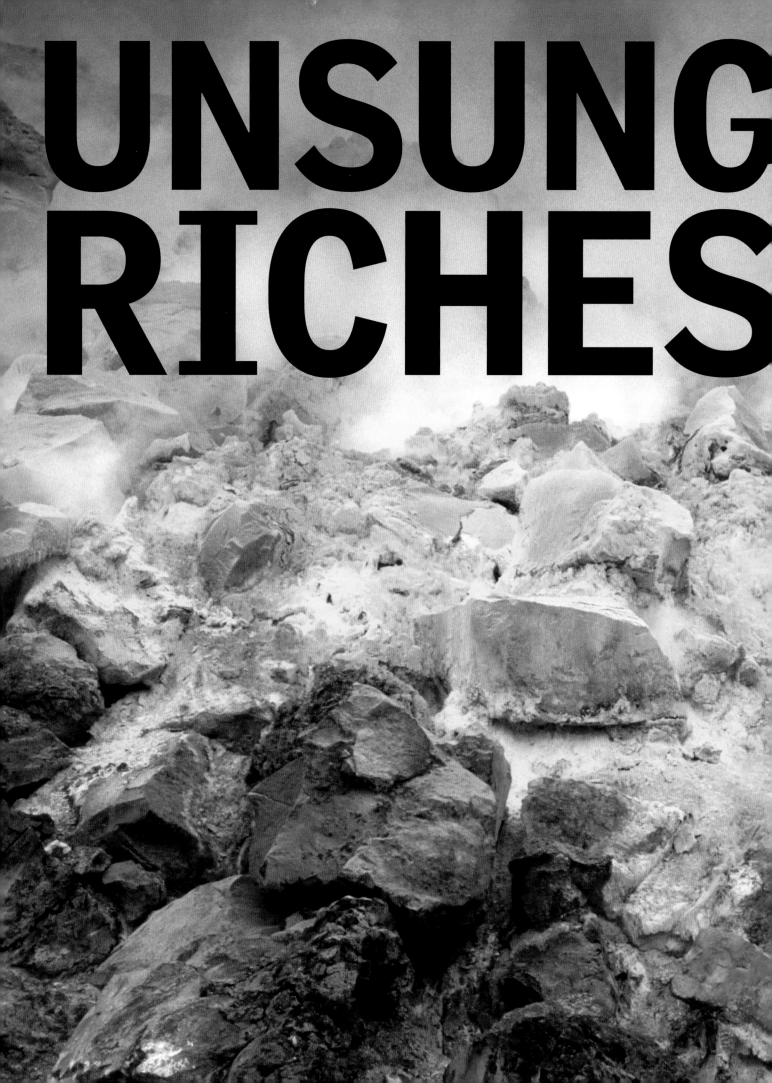

UNSUNG
RICHES

MANY OF THE MATERIALS WE NEED TO LIVE IN THE MODERN WORLD ARE MUCH LESS RARE THAN PRECIOUS METALS AND GEMSTONES BUT NO LESS IMPORTANT. There's the salt we use to preserve and add flavour to our food, the rock and concrete we use as the building blocks for construction, the clay we use to make both pots and high-tech advanced ceramics, and the silicon we use to make countless different items, from computer chips to contact lenses. There's also this bright yellow powder (left), which has erupted from vents inside a crater of the Sierra Negra volcano on Isla Isabela in the Galápagos Islands. Sulphur is one of the most important of the Earth's unsung riches, the bulk of it used to make sulphuric acid – a vital component of dyes, explosives, fertilisers, paints, plastics, textiles and many other useful materials.

SALT OF THE EARTH

MOST PEOPLE TAKE SALT FOR GRANTED, ADDING IT TO THEIR FOOD WITHOUT A SECOND THOUGHT. But there was a time when it was so important that it was seen as a measure of wealth. Countries that had a good supply of salt thrived, and one way that ancient civilisations, such as those of China, Egypt and Rome, became rich was by making, selling and taxing salt. The Romans even awarded their soldiers salt rations as part of their pay – the word 'salary' comes from the Latin *sal,* which means 'salt'.

The salt that we sprinkle on our food is made up of equal amounts of sodium and chloride. Individually, these two elements are highly poisonous, but when they combine they form a substance that is essential to life. In the days before refrigerators and freezers, it was particularly important as a preservative for food. People packed meat and fish with salt, and they used it to make butter and cheese from milk. It works as a preservative by drawing moisture away from the food and so preventing bacteria from multiplying. Thanks to salt, people could keep food for longer and travel greater distances on their own supplies.

Salt of seas and lakes

In the past, salt was costly because it was difficult to produce and transport. In ancient times, it was taken from salt flats along coastal regions, where salt had formed through the evaporation of seawater and could be scraped up from the ground. It was also harvested from dried-up desert lakes. In Ethiopia's Denakil Depression – one of the lowest and hottest places on Earth – this still happens. The depression is a vast salt plain, covering an area of some 1000 km^2, and even today the salt there is cut by hand into slabs, loaded onto mules and transported for sale throughout the Horn of Africa.

There is an abundance of salt in the sea, of course, but seawater needs to be boiled to evaporate the water, leaving the salt behind. This is costly in fuel, so people built

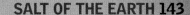

SALT MOUNTAIN So much salt is produced at the salt works on the island of Great Inagua in the Bahamas that the landscape resembles a series of snow-covered mountain peaks. This salt pan produces hundreds of tonnes of salt every year.

The waters of the Dead Sea, between Israel and Jordan, contain eight times more salt than normal seawater. Usable salt is produced there in shallow artificial ponds that are so vast they can be seen from space.

shallow inlet pools to trap seawater, which could be left to evaporate naturally in the Sun. There is evidence of salt works where this took place around the eastern and southern coasts of Britain. In Essex, for example, so-called 'red hills' can still be seen, large residues of red-coloured pottery, called 'briquetage'. This was used to make the shallow salt pans in which seawater was trapped then left to evaporate. The last of the water was driven off by boiling the salty water over a flame. The Domesday Book of 1086 lists more than 1000 salt works across Britain, at least 45 of which were in Essex. In 1394, the Guild of Salt Makers was established, reflecting the booming trade. Today, the Maldon Crystal Salt Company is the only salt business in Essex that still carries on the tradition of open-pan evaporation. The seawater, from the Blackwater Estuary, is heated in salt pans over a system of brick flues to create pyramid-shaped crystals of salt.

Although the production costs are low, making salt by evaporation is time-consuming and best suited to hot, sunny climates where the rate of evaporation is high. Today, most of the salt produced by evaporation comes from natural brines, in which the water contains a high concentration of dissolved salt to ensure a good yield. For example, the waters of the Dead Sea, between Israel and Jordan, contain eight times more salt than normal seawater. Usable salt is produced there in shallow artificial ponds that are so vast they can be seen from space.

SALT OF SUBSTANCE

THE WORLD'S OCEANS HAVE AN ALMOST INEXHAUSTIBLE SUPPLY OF COMMON SALT – SODIUM CHLORIDE, THE KIND WE USE IN OUR FOOD. Scientists think that there could be as much as 45 quadrillion tonnes (45 million billion tonnes) of it in seawater. That's enough to form a layer more than 150 m thick over the Earth's entire land surface. Although nowadays we get only a small proportion of our salt from the evaporation of seawater, that ocean supply is still the ultimate source of the salt we use.

Today, we get most of our salt from deposits of rock salt, called halite, or from natural brine springs. The rock salt formed as prehistoric seas, similar to the modern Dead Sea, that dried up millions of years ago leaving thick deposits of halite. These may now be found on or near the Earth's surface or buried deep under the ground. Often, they are mixed with sand that blew in as the seabed dried up. These impurities give salt deposits from particular locations their characteristic hues, which usually range from colourless to yellow, but can sometimes be light or dark blue or even pink.

Natural brine springs form when rainwater filters through deposits of rock salt, dissolving the salt crystals. This 'wild brine' can be pumped back up to the surface and then processed to extract the salt. Brine can also be created by pumping fresh water through layers of rock salt and collecting the salty water that is forced up to the surface.

Dancing amidst salt

Rock salt deposits are common throughout the world. They can stretch over vast areas, and they may be several hundred metres thick. Some of the most spectacular are those of the Wieliczka mine near Krakow in southern Poland. This is one of the world's

oldest operating salt mines – it has been worked since the 13th century – with more than 300 km of galleries, spread over nine separate levels. Over the centuries, workers have studded the walls of the galleries with statues sculpted in salt. Vast chambers, too, have been carved out, including a chapel and a ballroom complete with giant chandeliers. In the 17th century, kings and queens of Poland used to entertain guests with dancing in the ballroom and boat trips across underground lagoons of brine. The Wieliczka mine is now listed as a UNESCO World Heritage Site.

Today, the largest underground rock salt mine is at Goderich in Ontario, Canada. Extending 5 km beneath Lake Huron, the mine produces more than 7 million tonnes of rock salt each year. China and the USA are currently the world's leading producers of salt, but most countries are able to satisfy at least part of their needs with locally mined salt. Most of Britain's salt comes from the rich deposits that were discovered beneath Cheshire in 1670 and later in Worcestershire.

Essential for life

An average adult person has about 250 g of salt in his or her body. Like all mammals, we need it to regulate the body's fluid balance and maintain a healthy blood pressure. Nerves and muscles, including the heart, also rely on salt to work properly. Since we continually lose salt in our sweat and urine, we need to replenish our supply, but in fact most people take in more than they need. Adults require only about 6 g of salt per day – about a teaspoonful. We eat more partly because it tastes good, but mostly because processed foods, such as bread, ready meals, refined carbohydrates and sauces, contain a lot of hidden salt.

Only 1 per cent of the world's production of salt ends up on the dinner table. About half of global production is actually used to clear roads of snow and ice in the winter, which it does by lowering the freezing point of water. The rest is used in industry as a raw material for making

SALT MOUNTAIN Salt caves have been carved from the Muntanya de Sal (Mountain of Salt) at Cardona in Catalunya, Spain. Over the millennia, a salt layer buried under many kilometres of rock and mud pushed back up to the Earth's surface to form the mountain, or salt dome.

SALTY SCULPTURE Buried more than 100 m below the ground, St Kinga's Chapel lies in the heart of the Wieliczka salt mine near Krakow, Poland. Everything from the ornate sculptures to the grand chandeliers are shaped from the surrounding dark grey salt.

chemicals such as chlorine, sodium hydroxide and sodium carbonate. The industrial use of salt has its roots in the early 19th century, when the English chemist Sir Humphry Davy discovered how to separate a water solution of common salt into its constituent parts using electricity. Davy passed an electric current between two electrodes in the salt solution. He discovered that a pungent pale green gas, called chlorine, was released at the positive electrode. Hydrogen from the water was released as a gas at the negative electrode. Sodium remained in the solution to form sodium hydroxide.

At first, no one could think of anything useful to do with these substances, but subsequently they became the basis for many new industries. As a metal, sodium has many uses, such as in photography and the manufacture of strong steel alloys, detergents and dyes. Liquid sodium is also used in nuclear reactors as the coolant or heat exchanger. Sodium compounds include sodium carbonate, produced by passing carbon dioxide gas through a solution of salt and ammonia. This is used to make cosmetics, cleaning agents, degreasers, fire extinguishers, glass, metal fluxes, petroleum, soap and textiles. A by-product of sodium carbonate production is a compound called sodium bicarbonate, which is used as a raising agent in the baking industry and adds the sparkle to fizzy drinks such as cola.

The most important chlorine compound is hydrochloric acid, made nowadays by reacting sulphuric acid with salt, producing sodium sulphate as a by-product. Both hydrochloric acid and sodium sulphate are used in adhesives, ceramics, dyes, pigments, rubber, soap, textiles and many more products.

STRUCTURAL ROCK

FOR THOUSANDS OF YEARS, PEOPLE BUILT MOST STONE STRUCTURES FROM WHATEVER ROCK WAS CLOSE TO HAND. In many places around Britain, for instance, you can still recognise the underlying geology simply by looking at the local buildings and the materials from which they are made.

Examples include the silvery grey granite of Aberdeen, sparkling in the rare days of Scottish sunshine, and the honey-coloured limestone cottages of the Cotswolds. In Kent and Sussex, flint nodules stand out in the walls of cottages and churches, mined from the abundant local chalk, which on its own is far too soft for construction.

The builders of Petra in south-western Jordan, an Arab people called the Nabataeans, took this logic a step further – they simply carved their city out of the red sandstone cliffs. Petra is a hidden fortress, which can be accessed only through a narrow, winding passageway between sheer cliff faces called Al-Siq (the Shaft). Eventually, after about a kilometre, you reach its most famous monument, known as the Treasury (Al-Khazneh), although it was, in fact, a royal tomb. Numerous buildings with intricately carved façades make up the magical city, best viewed at dusk as the setting sun illuminates the sandstone in shades of orange and red.

EYE IN THE SKY This aerial view shows the landscape around Al-Deir (the Monastery), one of the cliff-face buildings at Petra, carved out by the Nabataeans 2000 years ago.

SANDSTONE SCULPTURES
Sculptures of gods and mythological creatures cover the façade of Petra's Al-Khazneh (the Treasury). They include female Amazon warriors and Medusa heads, carved directly out of the sandstone cliff.

Elsewhere in the world, stone or rock usually has to be quarried and then shaped into blocks before it can be used as a building material – stone treated in this way is called 'dimension stone'. It is taken from open-pit quarries or shallow, underground mines using various techniques, depending on the nature of the rock.

Hard rock, such as granite, for example, can be shifted using controlled explosions or by drilling a series of closely spaced holes into which iron wedges or inflatable pressure pads are inserted and the rock then levered free. Softer rock, such as limestone, may be cut with diamond wire, which slices off large, clean slabs, rather like a giant cheese-wire.

The slabs of rock or stone are then transported to a fabrication plant, where they will be cut to the required shape. Smaller brick-sized pieces, known as split stone, are used to construct and restore traditional houses. Thin stone slabs are produced for cladding, which adds attractive façades to municipal and commercial buildings. Any rubble produced during extraction and fabrication is usually broken up and sold as small rock chippings, called aggregate, which is an important ingredient of concrete.

Different dimensions

Granite, limestone, marble, sandstone and slate are the usual candidates for processing into dimension stone. Other rocks are chosen for their attractive texture or colour, such as alabaster, ironstones, onyx and serpentinite.

For new building work, architects and civil engineers choose a particular stone for its appearance, durability, strength and, of course, cost. In some cases it may be more economical to import dimension stone from a foreign quarry than pay for an expensive local stone. Restoration projects are different. In many countries, building regulations demand that new building materials used in restoration should be replaced 'like for like'.

ARTISTS' MATERIAL The marble quarries of Carrara in Tuscany, Italy, have yielded the stone for many famous Renaissance sculptures, including Michelangelo's David.

The extensive use of marble in the Taj Mahal – around 12 000 tonnes in the great dome alone – helps to make it the outstandingly beautiful monument it is. The building is especially magical at night, when the marble shimmers and glows in the moonlight.

In this case the stone must have the same physical and mechanical properties as the original stone, and it must also weather to the same colour. One type of stone can be specific to a particular region, or even to an individual quarry. If a quarry has closed, and the original building material is unavailable, the nearest substitute has to be sourced. This is why restoration work can often be extremely expensive.

One good way to see the variety of stones available in the British Isles is to visit the headquarters of the Geological Society in Burlington House, Piccadilly, London. The reception desk there is built from 17 slabs of popular building stones from Britain and Ireland: Lake District green slate, Connemara marble, Hurdcott stone (a pale green sandstone), Kentish ragstone (sandstone), Bath stone (limestone), blue lias (muddy limestone), Portland stone (limestone), Purbeck marble (muddy limestone), Hollington sandstone (red), Kilkenny marble (black limestone), Hopton Wood stone (limestone), Watts Cliff gritstone (sandstone), Woodkirk stone (sandstone), Caithness flagstone (lime-cemented sandstone), Shap granite (grey and pink), Corennie granite (red) and De Lank granite (light grey).

In fact, these are just a few examples of Britain's many local stones, and an almost endless variety of stone types are quarried and sold across the world. Certain countries are known for a particular type of stone. Some of the best marble, for example, is found in the Carrara marble quarries of Tuscany, Italy; Wales is famous for its rich purple slate; Brazil, Canada, China and India are known for their granites, and the USA produces some of the finest limestone. Consequently, dimension stone has become an international trade. The biggest market is the USA, where $3 billion was spent on dimension stone in 2005. Most of this was material imported from countries such as Brazil,

CALIFORNIAN CAPTAIN Carved over millions of years by glacial erosion, the sheer granite face of El Capitan (the Captain) rises over the forests of Yosemite National Park, California.

Canada, Italy and Turkey. Other important producers and exporters of dimension stone include China, India, Iran and Spain.

Marvellous marble

Luxury and quality are two words that sum up 'the king of rocks', valued for its fine grain, smooth texture and beautiful coloration. Marble is a metamorphic rock that forms when limestone recrystallises at high pressure and temperature beneath the Earth's surface. Normal limestone has natural cracks and fissures, but in marble the heat and pressure have created a hard, 'sugary' texture, ideal for shaping.

Great sculptors chose marble for statues such as the Venus de Milo. It adorns the floors, walls and ceilings of palaces, shrines and temples across the world, including the Taj Mahal in northern India. The Mogul emperor Shah Jahan completed the Taj Mahal in 1648 as a mausoleum for his favourite wife, who had died during childbirth. No expense was spared on the tomb, which represented the devotion he felt for his lost love. Pure white Makrana marble from quarries in Rajasthan covers the large domed structure and its four minarets. Both interior and exterior walls are lavishly encrusted with precious stones from all over the world – carnelian from Mesopotamia, crystal and jade from China, lapis lazuli from Afghanistan and onyx from Persia. The extensive use of marble – at least 12 000 tonnes in the dome alone – helps to make the Taj Mahal the astonishingly beautiful monument it is, especially at night, when the marble shimmers and glows in the moonlight.

Rock hard

Granite is an igneous rock that forms as molten material cools deep within the Earth's crust. It exists as vast bodies of rock, called batholiths, which can be several hundred kilometres across. Gradually, the granite is pushed up to the Earth's surface, or it becomes exposed through the forces of erosion.

The varied colour of granite depends on the minerals from which it is made – these include quartz, feldspar, mica and hornblende. Typical colours are pink, red, pale green, white or grey, and very rarely it takes on an attractive blue colour. The coarse grain size indicates that the rock has slowly cooled underground.

Granite is tough, hard and resistant to erosion. This makes it difficult to cut and carve but ideal for load-bearing masonry in construction. Since it forms such a range of colours, granite is also used for gravestones and as a facing stone in monuments, and it is a recent trend in kitchen worktops. Other common uses include windowsills and curbstones. Crushed granite is used as hard core for roads and other large construction projects.

Roofing stone

Slate is a metamorphic rock that starts life as a fine-grained clay or shale. Over time, high temperature and pressure deep beneath the Earth's surface compress the sediment, driving off all the water and aligning the minerals into parallel planes of weakness. This makes slate easy to split into thin sheets, or tiles. Since it is impervious to water, slate tiles are an ideal roofing and paving material. Welsh slate, which has been mined since Roman times, is highly prized. The Oakeley mine at Blaenau Ffestiniog was once the largest slate mine in the world.

THE CONCRETE JUNGLE

GRAVEL, ROCK DUST AND WATER – the raw materials don't sound exciting, but mix them together and the result is one of the strongest and most versatile of all building materials. A chemical reaction takes place when powdered rock, called cement, mixes with water. The cement gives off heat as it absorbs the water (hydrates) and begins to harden. Adding gravel or rock fragments (known as aggregate) to the mix results in an extra-strong material – concrete.

Test of time

The magic of concrete is that it is flexible and workable when wet, yet it sets into a hard material that gets stronger with time. It has a very long history. The Romans made it from volcanic ash, calcium oxide (quicklime) and pumice aggregate. They also sometimes added horsehair – to make the concrete set without shrinking – and blood to make it frost-resistant. One of the finest examples of their concrete engineering is the dome of the Pantheon in Rome, still standing today. Around 5000 tonnes of concrete were needed to make this perfect hemisphere, 44 m across. It would be an impressive structure even if it had been made in modern times, but it was built almost 2000 years ago. The fact that so many Roman buildings have stood the test of time is testament to concrete's durability. It has many other advantages as well. It insulates buildings from heat and sound;

BILLION-DOLLAR BRIDGE Confederation Bridge links Prince Edward Island with New Brunswick in Canada. Made from reinforced, post-tensioned concrete, the 12.9 km bridge is one of the longest in the world.

CONCRETE CITY Dubai in the United Arab Emirates has a booming construction industry. Many of the new concrete skyscrapers are centred around the tourist areas of Sheikh Zayed Road and Jumeirah Beach.

it can be formed into different shapes, and it does not catch fire. It has been used to build all sorts of structures, from bridges and dams to houses and skyscrapers.

In the mix

A typical modern concrete is a mixture of 41 per cent aggregate, 26 per cent sand, 16 per cent water and 11 per cent cement. Air makes up the remaining 6 per cent. The most widely used cement is Portland cement, invented in 1824 by Joseph Aspdin, a Yorkshire bricklayer by trade. It takes its name from its similarity to Portland stone, which was the most expensive building stone used in England at the time.

Portland cement is a combination of limestone mixed with shale, clay or mudstone, silica sand and iron ore. This material is ground up and heated to 1450°C in a large rotating kiln. The end product, called clinker, is mixed with about 5 per cent gypsum, a soft calcium-containing mineral, which gives builders enough time to pour and compact the concrete before it hardens. Blended cements can be made by grinding up Portland cement clinker and mixing it with other components, such as blast furnace slag, ash from coal furnaces or volcanic ash.

The choice of aggregate is vital, too. This usually consists of sand, crushed stone or gravel, but recycled waste, such as blast furnace slag, is also used. Aggregate increases the concrete's strength and lowers costs, since it is much cheaper than the same volume of cement.

In addition, various chemicals can be mixed in with the concrete to impart certain qualities. Accelerators, such as calcium chloride, speed up the hardening process to make a quick-setting concrete. Plasticisers – sometimes based on naphthalene, familiar as a key ingredient in mothballs – help to reduce the amount of water needed in the concrete mix, increasing the concrete's strength without

compromising workability. When it is used for load-bearing structures, concrete is usually reinforced with steel bars or mesh.

Another key process is 'curing' the concrete – keeping it moist and at a controlled temperature until it sets. This is important because the longer it stays moist, the stronger it will be when it does set. Ways of doing this include spraying surfaces with water or coating them in a sealant. Curing may take hours or days, depending on the type of concrete and the weather conditions.

Seeking 'greener' concrete

Making cement clinker gives off large quantities of carbon dioxide – roughly half a tonne for every tonne of cement produced. Overall, the cement industry produces around 5 per cent of global human-made carbon dioxide emissions, so a major challenge to manufacturers is to find fuel-efficient, non-polluting methods of producing cement. One growth area is the use of recycled materials to replace traditional clinker and aggregates. Manufacturers are also helping to reduce the impact on the environment by recycling water and concrete slurry.

Around 5000 tonnes of concrete were needed to make the dome of the Pantheon in Rome – a perfect hemisphere, 44 m across. It would be an impressive structure even if it had been made in modern times, but it was built almost 2000 years ago.

MATERIAL WORLD

THE RANGE OF MATERIALS THAT WE TAKE FROM THE EARTH'S CRUST TO TRANSFORM INTO USEFUL PRODUCTS IS ASTONISHING. Some, such as metal ores, coal or oil, are found only in a limited number of places, but others are far more commonplace. They are often widespread across the globe, yet just as important in our daily lives as any precious metal or gemstone. From the flint our forebears used to fashion early tools to the silicon used to make modern microprocessors, these materials have sometimes unexpected uses, and a few have helped to shape human civilisation.

Soft and scented

There is considerably more to the soft and soapy mineral called talc than the scented powder we use after a bath or shower. It is a form of magnesium silicate, found in magnesium-rich limestone (marble) or in the igneous rock that forms when molten material deep within the Earth's crust cools over a long period. Talc-rich rocks

SULPHUR LAKE A miner collects solid lumps of sulphur from the Ijen Crater in Java, Indonesia. Sulphur fumes escape from a volcanic lake in the middle of the crater and condense on rocks in vast quantities. The miners make an arduous four-hour trip on foot to collect lumps of sulphur and return carrying them in heavily laden baskets.

FINE PORCELAIN These small pellets of kaolin – a very pure form of white clay – will be used to make fine china in the famous porcelain factory at Sèvres, France.

include steatite or soapstone (where talc is found in a highly pure form) and blue schist, which contains talc mixed with other mineral impurities. Large talc deposits have been found in Austria, China, India, Korea, Syria and the USA.

In its purest form, talc has a lustrous white colour. It is extremely soft – in the Mohs scale of hardness (see box, below), it ranks lowest among all the minerals, with a hardness of just 1. It is so soft because it is composed of microscopic platelets that can easily slide over one another. It is also chemically unreactive and so holds fragrance well.

Many of the applications of talc reflect these properties. It is used to give paper a soft, smooth finish and it helps printing ink adhere evenly to the surface of the paper, improving the quality of printed images. In paint, talc adds a silky sheen to the surface of finished paintwork, allowing it to be wiped clean. It improves the opacity of white paint by dispersing the titanium dioxide pigment evenly through the paint, in this way also reducing the cost of production.

Fire and brimstone

In contrast to the whiteness of talc, sulphur is a bright yellow solid with fiery associations. It often exists in its native, or pure, form in the Earth's crust, but more frequently it combines with other elements to form compounds called sulphides and sulphates. Most sulphur is found near hot springs and volcanic regions, where it rises to the surface in the hot water; sulphur compounds are also found in fossil fuels, such as coal and natural gas.

Sedimentary deposits of sulphur can be mined at great depths using a method called the Frasch process, developed by the US engineer Herman Frasch in the 1880s. In this process, a system of three pipes is driven down a hole drilled into the deposit. Super-heated water is pumped down one pipe to melt the sulphur. Compressed air is pumped down the second pipe to provide pressure. This drives the molten sulphur up the third pipe to the surface, where it cools and hardens. Very pure sulphur is obtained in this way. Smaller amounts of sulphur are recovered from the compounds found in oil and natural gas.

The most common use of sulphur is in the production of sulphuric acid, one of the most important industrial chemicals, whose numerous applications range from dyes and car batteries to detergents and fertilisers. Millions of tonnes of sulphuric acid are made worldwide every year.

Clay and ceramics

Clay has been used both as a building material and in pottery since ancient times. This fine-grained sedimentary rock is made up of aluminium silicates that have weathered out of older rocks. There are many different types of clay, depending on the source rocks and local conditions. The familiar red and yellow bricks used to build houses are made from clay that has been fired at 1000°C in a kiln to make it stronger and more durable.

For hundreds of years, Chinese craftspeople have been making porcelain (or china) using a very fine and pure form of clay, rich in a mineral called kaolinite – after Gaolin in

---

MOHS SCALE OF HARDNESS

The Mohs scale is used to describe the hardness of a mineral by comparing it with other minerals. Devised by the German mineralogist Friedrich Mohs in 1812, it is a scale from 1 to 10, where 1 (talc) is the softest and 10 (diamond) is the hardest. Unlike the absolute hardness scale often used by scientists today, the steps between the grades in the Mohs scale are not equal. For example, diamond (10) is almost four times harder than corundum (9), which is twice as hard as topaz (8).

HARDNESS	SUBSTANCE OR MINERAL	ABSOLUTE HARDNESS
1	Talc	1
2	Gypsum	2
2.5–3	Pure gold	
3	Calcite, copper	9
4	Fluorite	21
4–4.5	Platinum	
5	Apatite	48
6	Orthoclase, titanium	
6–7	Glass, vitreous pure silica	
7	Quartz	100
7.5	Emerald, tungsten	
8	Topaz	200
9	Corundum, ruby/sapphire	400
10	Diamond	1500

SILICATE SHEETS Natural silicates form part of most rocks and many minerals, such as these flakes of sheet mica, called muscovite. Sheet mica is very important in the electronics industry, where it is used to make capacitors and electrical insulators.

Jiangxi province in southern China. In the 1750s, a similar kind of clay was discovered in Cornwall and called China clay or kaolin. Today, only a very small fraction of the kaolin mined from Cornish clay pits ends up as porcelain. Most is used as an additive in the paper-making industry, coating the sheets of paper to produce a soft finish that enhances the printing quality.

At the same time, modern advanced ceramics have found a range of other new applications, far removed from traditional chinaware cups and saucers. Advanced ceramics are incredibly tough, hard and heat-resistant materials, and their uses extend from abrasives and superconductors to military armour and electrical insulators.

Super silicon

After oxygen, silicon is the second most abundant element on our planet, making up 25 per cent of the Earth's crust. This amazing element is the basis for much of modern technology, from the microchips in computers to the tiles that form the heat shields on the space shuttles. Silicon's importance stems from being so abundant and the fact that it can form so many different types of molecule, making it an ingredient in a range of materials from sand to glass to plastic clay for children. Silicon is the most common material used in semiconductors, vital to the miniaturisation of modern computers and electronics equipment. Microchips, made from wafer-thin slices of ultra-pure silicon, can carry numerous tiny integrated circuits. Silicon is also an element in a group of advanced materials called silicones – plastics consisting of long chains of silicon, oxygen and organic molecules. One of their uses is in contact lenses, made from a soft silicone hydrogel, that are highly permeable to oxygen. This means that they can be worn for longer than other kinds of lens – up to 30 days of continuous wear.

TOOLMAKER'S ROCKS

Flint is a silicon-containing material that has been used since prehistoric times. Stone Age people learned that by hitting a flint with another stone or an animal bone – a technique called 'knapping' – they could fashion a sharp edge for use as a primitive axe, knife or scraper. An extremely hard form of the mineral quartz, flint was readily available – it is common throughout Europe and Asia and parts of Africa and the Americas. Although flint can be found as pebbles on beaches, the hardest and best-quality deposits occur as scattered nodules, lines and huge slabs within chalk (as in Dorset, right). These have to be dug out, and at Grimes Graves in Norfolk, discarded flint shards and chippings are the earliest evidence of prehistoric mine workings, dating back to 2500 BC. Using animal bones as wedges, Stone Age miners managed to dig down through the chalk until they reached the deposits. Some of these prehistoric shafts are 10 m deep, with horizontal galleries radiating off to follow the seams, testimony to the importance of flint as a material.

A MOST UNUSUAL MATERIAL,

GLASS FEELS LIKE A SOLID, BUT THE MOLECULES THAT COMPOSE IT ARE RANDOMLY ARRANGED, LIKE THOSE OF A LIQUID. It is this loose, random arrangement of molecules that makes glass transparent. But to think of glass as a liquid would be wrong. Its properties fall somewhere between those of solids and liquids – the fact that old leaded glass windows in churches are often thicker at the bottom is more to do with primitive glass-making techniques than the glass 'flowing' like a liquid.

Glass occurs naturally as obsidian. This opaque black glass forms when intense volcanic heat melts silica compounds in rocks which then rapidly cool in air. The black colour is due to high concentrations of iron oxide. Another type of natural glass, fulgurite, forms very occasionally when lightning strikes sand, fusing the silica in the sand as it ploughs into the ground.

Glass-making goes back thousands of years. The Romans produced some elaborate glass ornaments and the Egyptians used it to decorate the death masks of pharaohs. The craft of glass blowing (right) began in the 1st century BC in Syria. Venice became a centre for glass making, producing richly coloured ornamental glass and, from the 13th century, fine clear glass.

Today, glass is typically made from a mixture of about 75 per cent sand, 10 per cent limestone and 15 per cent soda ash. The raw materials are heated in a furnace until they fuse. The molten glass is poured, rolled or shaped and it then sets hard as it cools. By adding other minerals to the basic mix, the glass can be adapted for different purposes, from lenses and light bulbs to windows and windscreens. Glass is also used in advanced applications, such as composite materials and reinforced glass concrete.

NAME: Soda glass

COMPOSITION: Around 15 parts sand to 2 parts calcium carbonate to 3 parts sodium carbonate

SOFTENING POINT: Around 726°C

HARDNESS: 6–7 (Mohs scale)

DENSITY: 2.44 g/cm^3 (at 20°C)

ANNUAL GLOBAL PRODUCTION: More than 114.3 million tonnes

INDEX

A

aborigines 118, 119
Abu Simbel 83
Afghanistan 118, 125, 149
Africa 27, 47, 54–55, 56, 72–73, 76, 77, 101, 109, 111, 114, 115, 129, 132, 142, 154
agate 116
aggregate 150, 151
aircraft 97, 134, 135, 137
Akashi-Kaikyo bridge 132
alabaster 148
Alaska 23, 64, 65
albedos 20, 21
Algeria 69, 72–73
alloys 59, 94, 97, 104, 107, 109, 126–127, 132, 134, 137, 145
  uses for 126, 127
alluvial deposits 111
Alps 16
aluminium 30, 124, 127, 134–135, 136, 137, 138, 139
  aluminium oxide 135
  aluminium silicates 153
  uses for 134, 135
amalgams 99, 102
Amazonia 27, 98, 99
amber 119
amethysts 116
ammonia 69, 145
Amun, temple of 118
Andes 101, 122
animal life 23, 25, 27, 28, 61, 82, 83, 119
Antarctica 129
anthracite 58, 59
antimony 125
apatite 153
aphelion 18
AquaBuOY 89
aquamarine 116
aquifers 78, 79
Archimedes Wave Swing 89
Arctic 21, 23, 64, 70
Argentina 81, 91, 122–123
Arizona 75, 84, 85, 123
arsenic 125
Asia 54, 68, 77, 132, 154
asphalt 62
asphaltum 63
asthenosphere 37
Aswan High Dam 83
Atacama Desert 129
atmosphere 16, 18, 21, 40, 47
atomic power 48–51
  atomic bombs 48–49
Auranofin 97
aurora australis 40
aurora borealis 40, 41
Australia 27, 46, 47, 61, 72–73, 98, 100, 108, 111, 112, 116, 117, 118, 129, 131, 134, 135, 136

Austria 153
Azerbaijan 62–63, 66
Aztecs 108

B

bacteria 22, 25, 60, 63, 97
Bahamas 142–143
Baku 62–63
barium 139
barrages, tidal 86–87
basalt 38, 39, 100, 116
bauxite 134, 135, 138, 139
Becquerel rays 47
Beijing's Olympic stadium 120–121
Belgium 58
bell founding 126, 127
beryl 118
beryllium 137, 139
Bessemer process 132
Bilbao 136
biodiesel 56, 57
biodiversity 25, 27
biofuels 53, 56–57
biogas 57
biomass 57
biorefineries 56–57
Birmingham (England) 109
bituminous coal 58, 68, 131
Black Canyon 84, 85
Black Orlov diamond 112–113
Black Thunder Mine 60
Blackwater Estuary 143
Blaenau Ffestiniog 149
blowouts 62, 67
  see also gushers, oil
blueschist 153
boron 49, 113
borosilicate glass 47
Botswana 111
BP 68
brass 109, 127
Brazil 47, 57, 72–73, 81, 82, 99, 111, 116, 117, 118, 124, 131, 148
Brigham Canyon 106
brine springs 144
Bristol Channel 87
Britain 59, 60, 61, 68, 69, 104, 109, 119, 126, 143, 148
  see also England; Scotland; UK; Wales
bronze 104, 126–127, 130
  uses for 126, 127
Bronze Age 126, 127
brown coal 58, 59
bruting 114
Bulgaria 94
Bushveld Igneous Complex 109
butane 69

C

cadmium 49, 125
calcite 153
calcium 151
  calcium chloride 151
  calcium oxide 130, 150
California 31, 36, 43, 62, 63, 84, 98, 99, 149

California gold rush 99
California Institute of Technology 137
Camino Inca 123
Canada 23, 38, 40, 41, 46, 47, 59, 61, 72–73, 81, 87, 99, 111, 145, 148, 150–151
cancer 97, 106, 109
carats 94, 112, 113, 119
carbohydrates 56
carbon 23, 34, 54, 58, 63, 70, 102, 110, 113, 125, 130, 132
  carbon dioxide 20, 22, 25, 47, 54, 65, 68, 69, 70, 83, 130, 131, 135, 139, 145, 151
  carbon monoxide 61, 68, 131
  carbon nanotubes 30
carbonates 125, 145
Carboniferous period 58
carboplatin 109
carnelian 95, 149
Carrara marble 148–149
cars 56, 57, 62, 134, 135
  see also vehicles
Caspian Sea 66
cast iron 130
catalysts 106, 108, 109
cave paintings 124–125
cellulose 56
cement 150, 151
Centenary diamond 114
Central America 119
ceramics 153–154
chalk 146, 154
Chang Jiang 58, 75, 83
charcoal 54, 125, 130, 132
Chernobyl (1986) 47
Cheshire 145
Chile 107, 129
China 27, 58, 59, 61, 62–63, 67, 72–73, 75, 83, 87, 105, 108, 127, 131, 132, 145, 148, 149, 153, 154
  ancient 95, 130, 142
China clay 154
chlorides 142, 144, 151
chlorine 145
chlorofluorocarbons 22
chlorophyll 25, 27
chromium 118, 125, 132, 137
chromosphere 16
cisplatin 109
clay 38, 64, 123, 141, 149, 153–154
Cleopatra's mines 119
climate 25, 70, 76
climate change 16, 18, 21, 23
clinker 151
coal 34, 47, 53, 54, 57, 58–60, 61, 63, 68, 70, 72–73, 81, 131, 152, 153
Coalbrookdale 130
cobalt 125, 129, 132, 137
coins 95, 104, 108, 127
  see also currency
coke 58, 130, 131
Colombia 103, 116, 118
Colorado River 75, 84, 85

colours see pigments
Columbia River 81
comets 36, 128
compaction 39
computers 67, 95, 109, 139, 141, 154
concentrating solar power plants 28–29, 31
concrete 148, 150–151
Confederation Bridge 150–151
conglomerate 39
Congo, Democratic Republic of 81, 111
Congo, River 81
continents, movement of 37
convection 21
Convention on Biological Diversity 27
Coober Pedy 117–118
cooking 31, 42, 54, 57, 69, 107
copal 119
copper 30, 34, 94, 95, 97, 104, 106, 107, 109, 123, 124, 125, 126, 127, 137, 139, 153
  copper oxides 122
  copper sulphate 107
  uses for 107
coral reefs 24–25
core (of Earth) 36, 37, 40
Cornwall 127, 154
corona 16
corundum 118, 153
Costa Rica 72–73
Côte d'Ivoire 77
crops 27, 53, 56, 57
crown jewels 112, 115
crucibles 102–103
crust (of Earth) 36, 37, 46, 154
cryolite 135
crystals 93, 149
Cullinan diamonds 115
currency 95, 104, 106, 108, 127
Cyprus 107

D

dams, hydroelectric 75, 81, 82, 83, 84–85, 151
Danakil Depression 142
Danube, River 81
daylight 15, 18
Dead Sea 143, 144
Denmark 57, 91
dentistry 95, 97
desertification 54
deserts 20, 21, 23, 27, 38, 39, 62–63, 129
deuterium 50
Devon 87
Devonshire emerald 118
diamonds 110–115, 153
  cutting of 114–115
  legendary gems 112–113
  in space 113, 114
diatomite 45
diesel 62, 69, 70
dimension stone 148
dinosaurs 27, 58, 59, 129

diseases, waterborne 76, 77, 83
displacement of people 83
diversity 25, 60, 61
dolomite 131
Dominican Republic 119
Dorset 154
Dresden Green diamond 113
Dubai 151

E

Earth 16, 18–19, 20–27, 36–40,
    46, 154
Earth Summit (1992) 27
earthquakes 37, 44
Earthshine 21
eclipses, solar 15, 16
ecosystems 25, 27, 87
Ecuador 97
Edison, Thomas 59
Egypt 83
    ancient 95, 96, 107, 118, 128,
        142, 155
El Capitan 149
El Salvador 72–73
El Teniente 107
electricity 40, 95, 107, 109, 135, 145
    generation of 29, 31, 42, 43, 45,
        47, 48–49, 54, 57, 58, 59,
        69, 75, 81–91, 135
electromagnetic spectrum 20
electroplating 109
electrum 94, 104
emeralds 93, 116, 118–119, 153
emissions 54, 109, 151
endangered species 27, 83
energy 32–51
    energy conservation 97
    energy resources 72–73
    renewable 81, 83, 91, 107
    self-sufficiency in 57
    stored energy 52–73
    see also geothermal energy;
        hydropower; nuclear energy;
        solar energy; tidal power;
        wave power; wind power
England 18–19, 47, 54, 81, 86, 109,
    119, 151
EPNS (electroplated nickel silver)
    109, 127
equinoxes 18
erosion 39, 55, 83
Erta Ale 32–33
Essex 143
ethane 69
ethanol 56–57
Ethiopia 32–33, 142
ethylene oxide 108
Europe 31, 47, 57, 70, 71, 80, 81, 91,
    97, 109, 126, 127, 130, 132, 154
evaporation 78–79, 80, 142–143,
    144

F

farming 27, 55, 56
Federal Reserve Bank 104–105
feldspars 22, 149
fission 47, 48, 49

flares, solar 16
flint 152, 154
fluorite 153
fluxes 102, 131
forests 27, 54, 98, 99
Fort Knox 105
fossil fuels 22, 23, 25, 53, 54, 63,
    68, 70, 72, 83, 153
fossils 58, 59, 119
France 18, 30, 50, 57, 86, 87, 104,
    105, 108, 124, 125, 135, 153
Frasch process 153
fulgurite 155
furnaces 130, 131, 151, 155
fusion 16, 33, 34, 50–51, 155

G

Galápagos Islands 28, 140–141
gallium 139
Ganges, River 81
gas 34, 53, 54, 59, 65, 70
    natural gas 53, 62, 63, 68–71,
        72–73, 81, 153
        compressed natural gas 69
        liquified natural gas 68, 69
    town gas 68
gemstones 34, 113, 116–119, 141,
    152
    see also amber; emeralds; jet;
        opals; rubies; sapphires
Geological Society 148
geothermal energy 42–45, 72–73
Germany 61, 72–73, 91, 104, 105,
    127
geysers 42, 44
'The Geysers' power plant 43
Ghana 76
girdling 114
glaciers 16, 23, 76, 78, 129
glass 97, 153, 154, 155
    uses for 155
Global Mercury Project (GMP) 99
global warming 21, 83
glucose 25
gneiss 118
Gods 95, 96
Golconda diamond fields 111, 112
gold 33, 34, 93, 94–105, 106, 107,
    109, 123, 124, 134, 135, 139,
    153
    gold bullion 104–105
    gold reserves 104–105
    gold rushes 99, 101
    gold strikes 98–99
    industrial gold 100–101
    smelting of 102–103
    uses for 95, 96, 97
Golden Jubilee diamond 114, 115
Golden Pavilion (Kyoto) 96
Grand Canyon 75
granite 38, 39, 78, 99, 146, 148,
    149
    uses for 149
graphite 110
gravel 78, 150, 151
Great Inagua 142–143
Great Star of Africa (diamond) 115

Greece, ancient 80
Greek mythology 103, 135
greenhouse gases 22–23, 57, 70, 83
greenstones 100
greenswords 27
Grimes Graves 154
Guggenheim Museum (Bilbao) 136
gushers, oil 62, 63, 64
gypsum 93, 151, 153

H

habitat loss 27
hafnium 49
halite 144
hard coal 58
Hawaii 27
health resorts 61
heat 20, 36–37, 38–39, 78, 79, 155
    geothermal 42–43
    nuclear 47, 48
heating 45, 54
heavy-metal poisoning 125
heliostats 30
helium 16, 23, 34, 49, 50
Himalayas 37
Hiroshima 48, 49
HIV 97
Hoba meteorite 128–129
Hong Kong 105
Hoover Dam 82, 84–85
Hope diamond 113
hornblende 149
horseshoes 131
hydro-electric power see under
    hydropower
hydrocarbons 63, 64
hydrochloric acid 145
hydrogen 16, 23, 30, 34, 49, 50,
    63, 68, 145
    hydrogen bombs 49, 50
    hydrogen sulphide 69
hydrological cycle 78–79
hydropower 80–85, 135
    hydro-electric power 81–85
        see also tidal power; wave
            power
    microhydro power 83
hydrothermal activity 101, 108, 116
hydroxides 124

I

ice 38, 45, 76
    ice ages 18
    icecaps 23, 25, 78
Iceland 42–43, 45, 72–73
iguanas, marine 28
Iguazu Falls 81
Ijen Crater 152
ilmenite 136
Incas 94, 95, 123
India 31, 57, 59, 72–73, 95, 107, 111,
    112, 118, 131, 148, 149, 153
Indonesia 22, 72–73, 99, 152
Indus River 81
Industrial Revolution 59, 72, 80
infrared light 20, 21, 27, 96, 97
Inga Falls 81

ingots 102, 103, 105, 130
Iran 72–73, 149
Iraq 72–73, 107
Ireland 61, 148
iridium 94, 109
iron 22, 34, 36, 40, 94, 118, 124,
    125, 127, 128, 129, 130–131,
    132, 136, 137, 139
    iron ore 124, 130, 131
    iron oxides 123, 124, 125, 155
    smelting of 54, 59, 130–131, 132
    wrought iron 130, 131
Iron Age 130
iron-nickel 37
ironstone 22, 148
Islay 88
isotopes 47
Itaipú Dam 82
Italy 45, 72–73, 105, 125, 148–149

J

jade 149
Japan 16, 29, 42, 48, 67, 70,
    72–73, 105, 132
Java 152
jet 119
jewellery 95, 106, 108, 109, 112,
    113, 115, 136, 139
Johannesburg 102–103, 112
Joint European Torus (JET) 50–51
Jordan 146
Juma River 99

K

Kakadu National Park 46
Kalgoorlie 100
kaolin 153, 154
kaolinite 154
Kashmir 118
Kazakhstan 47, 72–73
Kenya 45
kerogen 62, 63
Khone Falls 81
Kimberley 111
kimberlite 111, 112
Klaproth, Martin 46, 135
Klondike gold rush 99
Koh-i-Noor diamond 112
Kono diamond fields 111
Korea 153
Kramer Junction 31
Kroll process 137
Kuwait 72–73
Kyoto 96

L

La Compania, church of 97
Lake Guatavita 103
Lake Mead 84, 85
Lake Myvatn 45
Lake Nasser 83
lakes 38, 39, 45, 76, 83, 84, 85,
    103, 152
    salt lakes 142
landfill 57
Laos 81, 99
lapis lazuli 95, 116, 125, 149

Lapland 47
Las Vegas 84, 85
Lascaux 125
Laugardalur 45
lava 33, 38, 39, 100
lead 34, 94, 124, 125
Leonid shower 128
Les Baux 135
Les Invalides 96
Lesser Star of Africa (diamond) 115
leucoxene 136
Libya 72–73
lichens 22
Lightning Ridge 117
lignite 58, 59
limestone 38, 39, 64, 122, 130,
   131, 146, 148, 149, 152, 155
lithosphere 36–37
Loch Linnhe 87
lodestone 130
London 16, 115, 135
Longyearbyen 18, 19
Los Angeles 103
Lucy (white dwarf) 113

M

McCabe Wave Pump 89
Macedonia 38
Madagascar 118
magma 38, 40, 42, 45, 110
magnesium 36, 137
   magnesium silicate 152
magnetism 16, 40, 50, 64, 130
magnetite 130
Mahamuni temple 96
malachite 116
Mali 55
manganese 123, 127, 132, 137, 139
   manganese oxides 125
mantle (of Earth) 36, 37, 39, 46
Maoris 42
marble 38, 39, 148, 152
martensite 132
medicine 25, 97
mercury 99, 102, 125
   mercury sulphide 125
Mesopotamia 126, 149
metallic glasses 137
metals
   metal ores 93, 122–125, 152
   modern 134–137
      see also aluminium; titanium
   precious 34, 106–109, 141, 152
      uses for 106
      see also gold; platinum; silver
   recycling of 138–139
   from space 128–129
   see also steel
Meteorite Hills (Antarctica) 129
meteorites 36, 114, 128, 129
methane 22, 57, 61, 68, 69, 70, 83
   methane hydrate 70
methanol 57
Mexico 72–73, 93, 108, 117, 119
mica 149, 154
microorganisms 25, 45, 53, 60,
   62, 63

Mid-Atlantic ridge 45
Middle Ages 80, 86, 109
Middle East 126
Mines Act (1842) 59
mining 61
   for bauxite 134
   for coal 53, 58, 59–60
   for copper 106, 107
   for diamonds 110–112, 115
   for emeralds 118–119
   for gemstones 116–119
   for gold 98, 99, 100–101, 139
   for opals 116–118
   open-cast 46, 60, 107
   prehistoric 154
   for salt 144–145
   for silver 108
   for uranium 46, 47
mirages 23
Mohs scale of hardness 136, 153
molybdenum 132, 136
Monument Valley 20–21
Moon 15, 16, 21, 86, 129
moonstone 116
Mount Fairweather Glacier 23
mountains 37, 39
mudlogging 67
mudstone 38, 39, 64, 123
Muntanya de Sal 144–145
Myanmar (Burma) 96, 116, 118
Myocrisin 97

N

Nagasaki 48
Naica Mine 92–93
Namib Desert 129
Namibia 23, 47, 72–73, 111,
   128–129
NASA 137
Native Americans 42, 63
neon 34
Netherlands 105
neutron bombs 49
Nevada 48–49, 84, 85
New Guinea 27
New Jersey 119
New York 59, 104
New York State 81
New Zealand 42, 45, 72–73
Niagara Falls 81
nickel 104, 109, 124, 129, 132, 137
   nickel silver 127
Niger 55, 72–73
Niger River 81
Nigeria 72–73
Nile, River 81, 83
nitrogen 23, 34, 69
nitrous oxides 22
Nizam diamond 111
nodding donkeys 62–63, 65
Norfolk 154
North America 27, 45, 68
North Pole 18
North Sea 66–67, 69
Northern Hemisphere 18, 19, 21, 40
northern lights 40
Northumberland 81

Norway 18, 19, 81
Notsuke Bay 16
Novvy Urengoy 71
nuclear energy 46–51, 72–73
   nuclear fission 47, 48, 49
   nuclear fusion 33, 34, 50–51
   nuclear reactors 47, 48, 50, 145
   nuclear waste disposal 47
Nullarbor Plain 129

O

obsidian 39, 155
Ocean Power Delivery 89
oceans 27, 76, 78, 79, 88–89, 101,
   144
Odeillo 30
oil 34, 53, 54, 57, 62–67, 68, 70,
   72–73, 81, 152, 153
   crude oil 62, 63, 67
   oil extraction 64–65
      from the seabed 66–67
   oil reservoirs 63–65
   oil rigs 66–67
   oil tankers 66–67
   surveying for 64–65
Old Faithful 44
Olympic Games 95, 120–121
Ontario 81, 145
onyx 148, 149
opals 116, 117–118, 119
Orange River 111
ores 39, 46, 47, 100, 102, 108,
   123, 124, 126, 130, 135, 136,
   137, 138, 139
   iron 124, 130, 131
   metal 93, 122–125, 152
Orkneys 86, 89
Ormuz 125
orthoclase 153
oscillating water column 88
oxides 22, 46, 47, 108, 122, 123,
   124, 125, 130, 135, 136, 150,
   155
oxygen 20, 23, 25, 30, 34, 36, 60,
   69, 70, 132, 135, 154

P

padparadscha 118
Painted Desert 123
Pakistan 118
palladium 94, 97, 109, 139
Pangaea 37
panning for gold 98–99
Pantheon 150, 151
Paraguay 82
Paraná River 81, 82
Pariah Canyon 39
Paris 96
Patricia emerald 118
peat 58, 60–61, 70
pegmatite 116
Pelamis 89
peridot 116
perihelion 18, 19
permafrost 70
Persia 149
Persian Gulf 125

Peru 18, 108
pesticides 27
Petra 146–147
petrochemicals 62
petrol 56, 62, 69, 70
pewter 127
Philippines 72–73
phosphor bronze 127
photosphere 16
photosynthesis 25, 27
photovoltaic cells see PV cells
phytobacteria 25
pig iron 131, 132
pigments 124–125
pipelines 64–65, 70, 71
pitchblende 46
placer deposits 101, 124
plankton 27, 62, 63
plants 22, 25, 27, 45, 53, 58, 60,
   61, 79, 82, 119
plasma 50
plastics 62, 108, 141, 154
plates (tectonic) 36, 37, 40, 42,
   45, 100
platinum 95, 97, 106, 107, 109,
   124, 139, 153
   uses for 109
plutonium 47
Poland 72–73, 104, 119, 144–145
porcelain 153–154
Portugal 89
potassium 37
   potassium carbonate 125
pottery, firing of 54
power plants 83
   coal-fired 59
   fusion 50
   geothermal 42–43, 45
   hydroelectric 81–85, 135
   natural gas 69
   nuclear 47, 48, 50
   solar 28–31
   tidal 86–87
   wave-powered 88–89
   wind farms 90–91
PowerBuoy 89
Precambrian period 122
precipitation 78–79
Premier Diamond Mine 115
propane 69
prospecting 62, 64–65, 98–99
Prudhoe Bay 64
pumice 150
PV cells 28, 29, 31

Q

quarrying 38, 148–149
quartz 119, 149, 153
Quaternary period 122
Quebrada de Humahuaca 122–123
quicklime 130, 150
Quito 97

R

radiation 16, 22, 47, 49, 113
radioactive decay 37, 47
radioactivity 47

radios, solar 31
rainbows 22, 23
Ramsar Convention (1971) 61
Rance estuary 86–87
recycling (of metals) 138–139
reflectance 20–21
reflection 22, 23
refraction 22, 23
renewable energy 81, 83, 91, 107
reservoirs 43, 63–65, 76, 78, 79,
      81, 82, 83, 84
residual deposits 124, 135
Reykjavik 45
Rhine Falls 81
rhodium 94, 109
Rift Valley 45
Rio de Janeiro 82
Rio Grande 123
rivers 16, 27, 38, 58, 59, 75, 76,
      78, 79, 80, 81, 82, 83, 84, 85,
      98, 99, 111, 123
rock 36, 37, 38–39, 63–65, 101
   igneous 38, 39, 116, 149, 152
   metamorphic 38, 39, 116, 118,
      149
   rock cycle 38–39, 116
   sedimentary 38, 39, 63, 116, 117,
      153
   structural 146–149
Rome, ancient 42, 104, 107, 142,
      150, 151, 155
Roussillon 124
rubies 93, 116, 153
Russia 47, 59, 61, 67, 69, 72–73,
      81, 109, 111, 118, 119, 131
rutile 136

S

Sahara 23, 129
Sahel 54–55
St Kinga's Chapel 145
salt 142–145
   rock salt 144
   salt mines 144–145
   uses for 145
San Andreas Fault 36, 37
sand 38, 151, 154, 155
sandstone 38, 39, 64, 78, 123, 148
   sandstone sculptures 146–147
Sanlúcar la Mayor 28–29, 31
São Paulo 82
sapphires 116, 118, 119, 153
satellite connections 67
Saudi Arabia 63, 67, 72–73, 81
Scotland 60–61, 87, 88, 89, 146
sea
   power from the 86–89
   salt from the 142–143, 144
seabed 38, 39, 88
Seaflow 87
seasons 18–19
Seattle's Central Library 132–133
sedimentation 39
seismic surveys 65
selenite 93
serpentinite 148
shale 149

Sheffield 109
Shetland 60–61
shooting stars 128, 129
Siberia 40, 52–53, 70, 71, 110–112
Siena 125
Sierra Negra volcano 140–141
silica 117, 153, 155
silicates 22, 130, 152, 153, 154
silicon 33, 34, 36, 127, 137, 141,
      152, 154
silver 46, 93, 94, 95, 97, 104, 106,
      107, 108–109, 123, 124, 139
   sterling silver 109
   uses for 108–109
slag 130, 131, 151
slate 39, 99, 148
Slepce quarry 38
smelting 54, 59, 102–103,
      130–131, 132, 139
Smoky River (Canada) 59
soapstone 153
soda glass 155
sodium 142, 145
   sodium aluminium fluoride 135
   sodium bicarbonate 145
   sodium carbonate 145
   sodium chloride 144
   sodium cyanide 102
   sodium hydroxide 145
   sodium sulphate 145
solar energy 15, 16, 20, 28–31, 86,
      88
solar flares 40
Solar System 34, 37, 129
solar wind 40
solstices 18, 19
South Africa 27, 47, 56, 72–73,
      101, 109, 111, 114, 115
South America 96, 103, 109
South Pole 18
Southern Hemisphere 21, 40
space
   diamonds in 113
   metals from 128–129
spacecraft 30, 136, 137, 154
spacesuits 97
Spain 28–29, 31, 91, 119, 130, 132,
      136, 144–145, 149
sports equipment 137
Sri Lanka 118, 119
Star of India (sapphire) 119
Star of Sierra Leone (diamond) 111
stars 34–35
steatite 153
steel 59, 121, 131, 132–133, 134,
      137, 138, 145
   uses for 132
Stingray 87
Stone Age 154
Stonehenge 18–19
sub-bituminous coal 58
submarines 135
sucrose 57
Sudan 99
sulphates 107, 145, 153
sulphides 69, 125, 153
sulphur 69, 141, 152, 153

sulphuric acid 145
   uses for 141, 153
Sun 14–31, 40, 49, 50, 78, 79, 80,
      86, 88
   eclipses of the 15, 16
   sunspots 16
sunlight 20–27, 53
   sunlight and life 24–27
superconductors 106
surveying (for oil) 64–65
Svartsengi power plant 45
Sweden 54
Switzerland 57, 81, 105
swords 130, 132
Syria 80, 153, 155

T

Taft (California) 62, 63
Taiwan 105
Taj Mahal 112, 148, 149
Taklimakan Desert 62–63
talc 152–153
Tanzania 99
tarpits 63
Taxco 108
tectonic activity 38
Thailand 96, 114, 118
Thames, River 16
thermal collectors 28–31
thorium 37
Thorne Moor 61
Three Gorges Dam 75, 83
Three Mile Island (1979) 47
tidal power 86–87
Tiffany & Co. 109
tin 126, 127, 130
titanium 118, 125, 134, 136, 137, 153
   titanium dioxide 153
   titanium oxide 136
   uses for 135, 136
Toledo 132
topaz 116, 153
tourmaline 116
Trans-Alaska Pipeline 64–65
trapiche 118
Triassic period 58
tritium 50
Trombe wall 29
tundra 52–53, 71
tungsten 132, 136, 153
Turkey 15, 104, 119, 131, 149
turquoise 95, 116
Tuscany 148–149
Tutankhamun, funeral mask of 95

U

UK 27, 61
   see also Britain
Ukraine 70, 71, 72–73
ultraviolet light 20, 96
UN 27, 145
Union Oil company 62
United Arab Emirates 72–73, 151
uranium 33, 34, 37, 46, 47, 48,
      72–73
   enrichment of 47
   uranium dioxide 48

uranium oxide 47
Urengoy 70, 71
USA 20–21, 22, 42, 47, 49, 56, 57,
      59, 60, 61, 63, 67, 70, 72–73, 81,
      84, 101, 104, 105, 108, 109, 117,
      119, 132, 139, 145, 148, 153
   US Department of Energy 137
Utah 20–21, 22, 39, 106
Uzbekistan 72–73
Uzhhorod 70, 71

V

Valdez 64
vanadium 118, 132, 136, 137
Varna 94, 95
vehicles 56, 69–70
   see also cars
Venezuela 72–73
Venice 155
Victoria Falls 81
viruses 25
volcanoes 37, 44, 111, 140–141,
      152, 153
   volcanic activity 38, 39, 42, 99,
      110, 116, 155

W

Wales 148, 149
water 74–89, 150, 151
   as a power source 80–89
      see also hydropower; tidal
         power; wave power
   as a resource 76–77
WaterAid 76
Wave Dragon 89
wave power 88–89
weather systems 20, 21–23
weathering 20, 21–22, 39, 135
Weipa bauxite mine 134
Whitby 119
white dwarfs 113
Wieliczka mine 144–145
wind 20, 21, 38, 88
wind power 75, 90–91
Witwatersrand basin 101
wood 53, 54–55, 70, 125
World Energy Council 81, 90, 91
World Gold Council 95, 105
World Heritage Site 145
Wyoming 60

Y

Yamal Peninsula 70
Yangtze River 27, 58, 75, 83
Yellowstone National Park 44, 101
Yosemite National Park 149

Z

Zambezi River 81
Zambia 81, 118
Zimbabwe 81, 99, 118
zinc 97, 109, 124, 127, 137, 139
zirconium 137
Zoological Society of London 27

PICTURE CREDITS

NATURE'S MIGHTY POWERS: EARTH'S RICHES
was published by The Reader's Digest Association Ltd,
London. It was created and produced for Reader's Digest
by Toucan Books Ltd, London.

The Reader's Digest Association Ltd,
11 Westferry Circus,
Canary Wharf,
London E14 4HE
www.readersdigest.co.uk

First edition copyright © 2008

Written by
Celia Coyne

FOR TOUCAN BOOKS

Editors Jane Chapman, Helen Douglas-Cooper,
Andrew Kerr-Jarrett
Designers Bradbury & Williams
Picture researchers Wendy Brown, Sharon Southern,
Mia Stewart-Wilson, Christine Vincent
Proofreader Marion Dent
Indexer Michael Dent

FOR READER'S DIGEST

Project editor Christine Noble
Art editor Julie Bennett
Pre-press account manager Penny Grose
Product production manager Claudette Bramble
Production controller Katherine Bunn

READER'S DIGEST, GENERAL BOOKS

Editorial director Julian Browne
Art director Anne-Marie Bulat

Colour origination Colour Systems Ltd, London
Printed and bound in China